lonely planet

Fast Talk

Latin American
Spanish

Guaranteed to get you talking

Contents

⇒ Special Features

Before You Go

Although it is possible to get by in major Latin American cities without speaking Spanish, just a few phrases go a long way in making friends, inviting service with a smile, and ensuring a rich and rewarding travel experience – you could dance the night away at a salsa club, taste the best local dishes or find a gorgeous beach off the tourist trail.

PRONUNCIATION TIPS

The sounds of Spanish can almost all be found in English, and if you read our coloured pronunciation guides as if they were English you'll be understood. The stressed syllables are indicated with italics.

★ The few sounds that do differ from English include the strong and rolled r, and the harsh and throaty kh (as in the Scottish *loch*).

★ Also note that the Spanish v is soft, pronounced almost like a 'b' (with the lips pressed together), and that *ll* is generally pronounced as the 'y' in 'yes' (see also p65).

★ If you're familiar with the sound of European Spanish, you'll notice that Latin Americans don't 'lisp' – ie the European Spanish th is pronounced as s in Latin America.

MUST-KNOW GRAMMAR

The structure of Spanish holds no major surprises for English speakers since the two languages are quite closely related.

★ Spanish has a formal and informal word for 'you' (*Usted* oo·*ste* and *tú* too respectively). When talking to someone familiar or younger than you, use the informal *tu* form.

Phrases in this book use the form that is appropriate to the situation. Where both forms can be used, they are indicated by **pol** and **inf** respectively. Note that in some countries you may hear *vos* vos used instead of *tú*.

★ Spanish distinguishes between masculine and feminine forms of words, eg *bello/bella* be·yo/be·ya (beautiful), indicated in this book by **m** and **f**.

★ Verbs have a different ending for each person, like the English 'I do' vs 'he/she do**es**'. Travellers don't need to worry too much about this though – if you use the dictionary form of a verb in all contexts, you'll still be understood.

REGIONAL VARIATION

Influenced by indigenous languages, Latin American Spanish varies slightly from country to country, especially when it comes to vocabulary. In this book country-specific terms are indicated with abbreviations (see p95).

Fast Talk Spanish

Don't worry if you've never learnt Spanish (*español* es·pa·nyol), or Castilian (*castellano* kas·te·lya·no) as it's also called, before – it's all about confidence. You don't need to memorise endless grammatical details or long lists of vocabulary – you just need to start speaking. You have nothing to lose and everything to gain when the locals hear you making an effort. And remember that body language and a sense of humour have a role to play in every culture.

"you just need to start speaking"

Even if you use the very basics, such as greetings and civilities, your travel experience will be the better for it. Once you start, you'll be amazed how many prompts you'll get to help you build on those first words. You'll hear people speaking, pick up sounds and expressions from the locals, catch a word or two that you know from TV already, see something on a billboard – all these things help to build your understanding.

5

5. Phrases to Learn Before You Go

1. Can you recommend private lodgings?
¿Puede recomendar una casa particular?
pwe·de re·ko·men·dar oo·na ka·sa par·tee·koo·lar

Staying with locals will give you a true Cuban experience and an opportunity to sample hearty home-cooked dishes.

2. I'd like the fixed-price menu, please.
Quisiera el menú del día, por favor.
kee·sye·ra el me·noo del dee·a por fa·vor

Eateries in Guatemala and Mexico usually offer a fixed-price meal which may include up to four courses and is great value.

3. Where can I get a shared taxi/minibus?
¿Dónde se puede tomar un colectivo?
don·de se pwe·de to·mar oon ko·lek·tee·vo

Cheap transport options in Peru and other countries are shared taxis or minibuses – ask locally as there are no obvious stops.

4. Where can we go salsa/tango dancing?
¿Dónde podemos ir a bailar salsa/tango?
don·de po·de·mos eer a bai·lar sal·sa/tan·go

In dance-crazy Colombia and Argentina you won't be lacking in dance-hall options, but you may want a local recommendation

5. How do you say ... in your language?
¿Cómo se dice ... en su lengua?
ko·mo se dee·se ... en su len·gwa

Among hundreds of indigenous languages in Latin America are Quechua, Aymara, Mayan languages, Náhuatl and Guaraní.

10. Phrases to Sound Like a Local

BEFORE YOU GO

| What's up? | **¿Qué más?** (Col) | ke mas |

| What's up? | **¿Qué bolá asere?** (Cub) | ke bo·*la* a·se·re |

| Cool! | **¡Chévere!** (Col/Ven) | *che*·ve·re |

| How cool! | **¡Qué chido!** (Mex) | ke *chee*·do |

| No problem. | **No hay drama.** | no ai *dra*·ma |

| Get on with it! | **¡Ponte las pilas!** (Arg) | *pon*·te las *pee*·las |

| It's messed up. | **Está en llama.** (Cub) | es·*ta* en *ya*·ma |

| Come off it! | **¡No manches!** (Mex) | no *man*·ches |

| No way! | **¡Ni hablar!** (Arg) | nee a·*blar* |

| Of course! | **¡Claro!** | *kla*·ro |

7

10. Phrases to Start a Sentence

When's (the last flight)?	¿Cuándo sale (el último vuelo)? *kwan·do sa·le (el ool·tee·mo vwe·lo)*
Where's (the station)?	¿Dónde está (la estación)? *don·de es·ta (la es·ta·syon)*
How much is (the room)?	¿Cuánto cuesta (la habitación)? *kwan·to kwes·ta (la a·bee·ta·syon)*
I'm looking for (a hotel).	Estoy buscando (un hotel). *es·toy boos·kan·do (oon o·tel)*
Do you have (a map)?	¿Tiene (un mapa)? *tye·ne (oon ma·pa)*
Is there (a toilet)?	¿Hay (un baño)? *ai (oon ba·nyo)*
I'd like (a coffee).	Quisiera (un café). *kee·sye·ra (oon ka·fe)*
Can I (enter)?	¿Se puede (entrar)? *se pwe·de (en·trar)*
Can you please (help me)?	¿Puede (ayudarme), por favor? *pwe·de (a·yoo·dar·me) por fa·vor*
Do I have to (book)?	¿Necesito (reservar)? *ne·se·see·to (re·ser·var)*

Chatting & Basics

≡ Fast Phrases

Hello./Goodbye.	Hola./Adiós. o·la/a·*dyos*
Please./Thank you.	Por favor./Gracias. por fa·*vor*/*gra*·syas
Do you speak English?	¿Habla/Hablas inglés? pol/inf *a*·bla/*a*·blas een·*gles*

Essentials

Yes./No.	Sí./No. see/no
Please.	Por favor. por fa·*vor*
Thank you (very much).	(Muchas) Gracias. (*moo*·chas) *gra*·syas
You're welcome.	De nada. de *na*·da Con mucho gusto. **(CAm)** kon *moo*·cho *goo*·sto
Excuse me.	Disculpe. dees·*kool*·pe Con permiso. **(CAm)** kon per·*mee*·so

| Sorry. | Perdón. |
| | per·*don* |

Language Difficulties

Do you speak English?	¿Habla/Hablas inglés? pol/inf
	a·bla/*a*·blas een·*gles*
Does anyone speak English?	¿Hay alguien que hable inglés?
	ai al·*gyen* ke *a*·ble een·*gles*
Do you understand?	¿Me entiende/ entiendes? pol/inf
	me en·*tyen*·de/en·*tyen*·des
I don't understand.	No entiendo.
	no en·*tyen*·do
I speak a little.	Hablo un poco.
	a·blo oon *po*·ko
What does ... mean?	¿Qué significa ...?
	ke seeg·nee·*fee*·ka ...
How do you pronounce this?	¿Como se pronuncia esto?
	ko·mo se pro·*noon*·sya *es*·to
How do you write ...?	¿Como se escribe ...?
	ko·mo se es·*kree*·be ...
Could you please repeat that?	¿Puede repetirlo, por favor?
	pwe·de re·pe·*teer*·lo por fa·*vor*
Could you please write it down?	¿Puede escribirlo, por favor?
	pwe·de es·kree·*beer*·lo por fa·*vor*
Could you please speak more slowly?	¿Puede hablar más despacio, por favor?
	pwe·de a·*blar* mas des·*pa*·syo por fa·*vor*
✂ Slowly, please!	¡Despacio, por favor!
	des·*pa*·syo por fa·*vor*

Greetings

Hello./Hi.	Hola.
	o·la
	¿Qué hubo? (Chi)
	ke oo·bo
Good morning.	Buenos días.
	bwe·nos dee·as
Good afternoon.	Buenas tardes.
	bwe·nas tar·des
Good evening/night.	Buenas noches.
	bwe·nas no·ches
See you later.	Hasta luego.
	as·ta lwe·go
Goodbye.	Adiós.
	a·dyos
Bye.	Chao.
	chow
How are you?	¿Cómo está? sg pol
	ko·mo es·ta
	¿Cómo estás? sg inf
	ko·mo es·tas
	¿Cómo están? pl
	ko·mo es·tan

Fast Talk **Greetings**

Never address a stranger or approach people for information without extending a greeting such as *buenos días* bwe·nos dee·as (good morning) or *buenas tardes* bwe·nas tar·des (good afternoon). It's also polite to greet the assembled company when entering a public place such as a shop or a cafe.

Fine, thank you.	Bien, gracias.
And you?	¿Y Usted/tú? pol/inf
	byen *gra*·syas
	ee oos·*te*/too

Titles

Mr	Señor
	se·*nyor*
Mrs/Ms	Señora
	se·*nyo*·ra
Miss	Señorita
	se·nyo·*ree*·ta

Introductions

What's your name?	¿Cómo se llama Usted? pol
	ko·mo se *ya*·ma oos·*te*
	¿Cómo te llamas? inf
	ko·mo te *ya*·mas
My name is ...	Me llamo ...
	me *ya*·mo ...
I'm pleased to meet you.	Mucho gusto.
	moo·cho *goos*·to

Fast Talk **Addressing People**

Women are mostly addressed as *Señora* se·*nyo*·ra regardless of age or marital status, though some older unmarried women may prefer to be called *Señorita* se·nyo·*ree*·ta. Men are usually addressed as *Señor* se·*nyor*. *Doña do*·nya, although rare, is used as a mark of respect towards older women, while *Don* don is sometimes used to address men.

It's been great meeting you.	Me ha encantado conocerle/conocerte. **pol/inf**	me a en·kan·*ta*·do ko·no·*ser*·le/ko·no·*ser*·te
I'd like to introduce you to ...	Quisiera presentarle/te a ... **pol/inf**	kee·*sye*·ra pre·sen·*tar*·le/te a ...
✂ **This is ...**	Éste/Ésta es ... **m/f**	*es*·te/*es*·ta es ...

PHRASE BUILDER

This is my ...	Éste/Ésta es mi ... **m/f**	*es*·te/*es*·ta es mee ...
child	hijo/a **m/f**	ee·*kho*/a
colleague	colega	ko·*le*·ga
friend	amigo/a **m/f**	a·*mee*·go/a
husband	esposo	es·*po*·so
partner	pareja	pa·*re*·kha
wife	esposa	es·*po*·sa

What's your ...? ¿Cuál es tu ...?
kwal es too ...

PHRASE BUILDER

Here's my ...	Ésta es mi ...	*es*·ta es mee ...
address	dirección	dee·rek·*syon*
email address	dirección de email	dee·rek·*syon* de ee·mayl
mobile number	número de celular	*noo*·me·ro de se·loo·*lar*
phone number	número de teléfono	*noo*·mero de te·*le*·fo·no

13

Personal Details

Where are you from?	¿De dónde es/eres? pol/inf
	de *don*·de es/*e*·res

PHRASE BUILDER

I'm from ...	Soy de ...	soy de ...
Australia	Australia	ow·*stra*·lya
Canada	Canadá	ka·na·da
England	Inglaterra	een·gla·*te*·ra
New Zealand	Nueva Zelanda	*nwe*·va se·*lan*·da
the USA	los Estados Unidos	los es·*ta*·dos oo·*nee*·dos

Are you married?	¿Está casado/a? m/f pol
	es·*ta* ka·*sa*·do/a
	¿Estás casado/a? m/f inf
	es·*tas* ka·*sa*·do/a
I'm single.	Soy soltero/a. m/f
	soy sol·*te*·ro/a
I'm married.	Estoy casado/a. m/f
	es·*toy* ka·*sa*·do/a
I'm separated.	Estoy separado/a. m/f
	es·*toy* se·pa·*ra*·do/a

Age

How old are you?	¿Cuántos años tiene/tienes? pol/inf
	kwan·tos *a*·nyos *tye*·ne/*tye*·nes
I'm ... years old.	Tengo ... años.
	ten·go ... *a*·nyos

14

How old is your son?	¿Cuántos años tiene su/tu hijo? pol/inf
	kwan·tos a·nyos tye·ne soo/too ee·kho
How old is your daughter?	¿Cuántos años tiene su/tu hija? pol/inf
	kwan·tos a·nyos tye·ne soo/too ee·kha
He/She is ... years old.	Tiene ... años.
	tye·ne ... a·nyos

Occupations & Study

What's your occupation?	¿A qué se dedica? pol
	a ke se de·dee·ka
	¿A qué te dedicas? inf
	a ke te de·dee·kas
I'm (an office worker).	Soy (oficinista).
	soy (o·fee·see·nee·sta)
I work in (education).	Trabajo en (enseñanza).
	tra·ba·kho en (en·se·nyan·sa)
I work in (hospitality).	Trabajo en (hostelería).
	tra·ba·kho en (os·te·le·ree·a)
I'm self-employed.	Soy trabajador/trabajadora autónomo/a. m/f
	soy tra·ba·kha·dor/ tra·ba·kha·do·ra ow·to·no·mo/a
I'm retired.	Estoy jubilado/a. m/f
	es·toy khoo·bee·la·do/a
I'm unemployed.	Estoy desempleado/a. m/f
	es·toy des·em·ple·a·do/a
I'm a student.	Soy estudiante.
	soy es·too·dyan·te

15

What are you studying?	¿Qué estudia/estudias? pol/inf ke es·*too*·dya/es·*too*·dyas
I'm studying languages.	Estudio idiomas. es·*too*·dyo ee·*dyo*·mas
I'm studying science.	Estudio ciencias. es·*too*·dyo *syen*·syas

Interests

What do you do in your spare time?	¿Qué te gusta hacer en tu tiempo libre? ke te *goos*·ta a·*ser* en too *tyem*·po *lee*·bre
Do you like (art)?	¿Te gusta (el arte)? te *goos*·ta (el *ar*·te)
Do you like (sport)?	¿Te gustan (los deportes)? te *goos*·tan (los de·*por*·tes)
I like (music).	Me gusta (la música). me *goos*·ta (la *moo*·see·ka)
I like (films).	Me gusta (el cine). me *goos*·ta (el *see*·ne)
I don't like (cooking).	No me gusta (cocinar). no me *goos*·ta (ko·see·*nar*)
I don't like (hiking).	No me gusta (el excursionismo). no me *goos*·ta (el eks·koor·syo·*nees*·mo)

Feelings

| Are you ...? | ¿Tiene/Tienes ...? pol/inf
tye·ne/*tye*·nes ... |

PHRASE BUILDER

I'm (not) ...	(No) Tengo ...	(no) ten·go ...
cold	frío	free·o
hot	calor	ka·lor
hungry	hambre	am·bre
in a hurry	prisa	pree·sa
thirsty	sed	se

Are you ...?	¿Está/Estás ...? pol/inf
	es·ta/es·tas ...

PHRASE BUILDER

I'm (not) ...	(No) Estoy ...	(no) es·toy ...
happy	feliz	fe·lees
sad	triste	trees·te
tired	cansado/a m/f	kan·sa·do/a
well	bien	byen

Numbers

1	uno	oo·no
2	dos	dos
3	tres	tres
4	cuatro	kwa·tro
5	cinco	seen·ko
6	seis	says
7	siete	sye·te
8	ocho	o·cho
9	nueve	nwe·ve
10	diez	dyes

11	once	*on*·se
12	doce	*do*·se
13	trece	*tre*·se
14	catorce	ka·*tor*·se
15	quince	*keen*·se
16	dieciséis	dye·see·*says*
17	diecisiete	dye·see·*sye*·te
18	dieciocho	dye·see·*o*·cho
19	diecinueve	dye·see·*nwe*·ve
20	veinte	*vayn*·te
21	veintiuno	vayn·tee·*oo*·no
30	treinta	*trayn*·ta
40	cuarenta	kwa·*ren*·ta
50	cincuenta	seen·*kwen*·ta
60	sesenta	se·*sen*·ta
70	setenta	se·*ten*·ta
80	ochenta	o·*chen*·ta
90	noventa	no·*ven*·ta
100	cien	*syen*
200	doscientos	dos·*syen*·tos
1000	mil	*meel*
1,000,000	un millón	oon mee·*yon*

Time

What time is it?	¿Qué hora es?
	ke *o*·ra es
It's one o'clock.	Es la una.
	es la *oo*·na

Fast Talk — Telling the Time

Both the 12-hour and the 24-hour clocks are commonly used when telling the time in Spanish. 'It is ...' is expressed by *Son las* ... son las ..., followed by a number, but 'one o'clock' is *Es la una* es la *oo*·na. For times after the half hour, say the next hour 'minus' (*menos me*·nos) the minutes until that hour arrives, eg '20 to eight' is *las ocho menos veinte* las *o*·cho *me*·nos *vayn*·te. For times after the hour, use 'and' (*y* ee), eg '20 past eight' is *las ocho y veinte* las *o*·cho ee *vayn*·te.

It's (10) o'clock.	Son las (diez). son las (dyes)
Quarter past (two).	(Las dos) y cuarto. (las dos) ee *kwar*·to
Half past (two).	(Las dos) y media. (las dos) ee *me*·dya
Quarter to (three).	(Las tres) menos cuarto. (las *tres*) *me*·nos *kwar*·to
At what time ...?	¿A qué hora ...? a ke *o*·ra ...
At one o'clock.	A la una. a la *oo*·na
At (six) o'clock.	A las (seis). a las (says)
in the morning	por la mañana por la ma·*nya*·na
in the afternoon	por la tarde por la *tar*·de
in the evening	por la noche por la *no*·che

Days

Monday	lunes m	*loo*·nes
Tuesday	martes m	*mar*·tes
Wednesday	miércoles m	*myer*·ko·les
Thursday	jueves m	*khwe*·ves
Friday	viernes m	*vyer*·nes
Saturday	sábado m	*sa*·ba·do
Sunday	domingo m	do·*meen*·go

Months

January	enero m	e·*ne*·ro
February	febrero m	fe·*bre*·ro
March	marzo m	*mar*·so
April	abril m	a·*breel*
May	mayo m	*ma*·yo
June	junio m	*khoon*·yo
July	julio m	*khool*·yo
August	agosto m	a·*gos*·to
September	septiembre m	sep·*tyem*·bre
October	octubre m	ok·*too*·bre
November	noviembre m	no·*vyem*·bre
December	diciembre m	dee·*syem*·bre

Dates

What date?	¿Qué fecha?
	ke *fe*·cha
What's today's date?	¿Qué día es hoy?
	ke *dee*·a es oy

Fast Talk Starting Off

When starting to speak another language, your biggest hurdle is saying aloud what may seem to be just a bunch of sounds. The best way to do this is to memorise a few key words, like 'hello', 'thank you' and 'how much?', plus at least one phrase that's not essential, eg 'how are you', 'see you later' or 'it's very cold/hot' (people love to talk about the weather!). This will enable you to make contact with the locals, and when you get a reply and a smile, it'll also boost your confidence.

It's (18 October).	Es (el dieciocho de octubre). es (el dye·see·o·cho de ok·too·bre)
yesterday morning	ayer por la mañana a·yer por la ma·nya·na
tomorrow morning	mañana por la mañana ma·nya·na por la ma·nya·na
yesterday afternoon	ayer por la tarde a·yer por la tar·de
tomorrow afternoon	mañana por la tarde ma·nya·na por la tar·de
yesterday evening	ayer por la noche a·yer por la no·che
tomorrow evening	mañana por la noche ma·nya·na por la no·che
last week	la semana pasada la se·ma·na pa·sa·da
next week	la semana próxima la se·ma·na prok·see·ma
last month	el mes pasado el mes pa·sa·do

next month	el mes próximo
	el mes *prok*·see·mo
last year	el año pasado
	el *a*·nyo pa·*sa*·do
next year	el año próximo
	el *a*·nyo *prok*·see·mo

Weather

What's the weather like?	¿Qué tiempo hace?
	ke *tyem*·po a·se
What's the weather forecast?	¿Cuál es el pronóstico del tiempo?
	kwal es el pro·*nos*·tee·ko del *tyem*·po
It's raining.	Llueve.
	(oy) *ywe*·ve
It's snowing.	Nieva.
	(oy) *nye*·va

PHRASE BUILDER

It's ...	Hace ...	*a*·se ...
(very) cold	(mucho) frío	(*moo*·cho) *free*·o
sunny	sol	sol
warm	calor	ka·*lor*
windy	viento	*vyen*·to

Directions

| **Where's (the bank)?** | ¿Dónde está (el banco)? |
| | *don*·de es·*ta* (el *ban*·ko) |

Which way is (the post office)?	¿Por dónde se va a (correos)? por *don*·de se va a (ko·*re*·os)
What's the address?	¿Cuál es la dirección? kwal es la dee·rek·*syon*
Can you please write it down?	¿Puede escribirlo, por favor? *pwe*·de es·kree·*beer*·lo por fa·*vor*
Can you show me (on the map)?	¿Me lo podría indicar (en el mapa)? me lo po·*dree*·a een·dee·*kar* (en el *ma*·pa)
How far is it?	¿A cuánta distancia está? a *kwan*·ta dees·*tan*·sya es·*ta*
Turn at the corner.	Doble en la esquina. *do*·ble en la es·*kee*·na
Turn at the traffic lights.	Doble en el semáforo. *do*·ble en el se·*ma*·fo·ro
Turn left.	Doble a la izquierda. *do*·ble a la ees·*kyer*·da
Turn right.	Doble a la derecha. *do*·ble a la de·*re*·cha
behind ...	detrás de ... de·*tras* de ...
in front of ...	adelante de ... a·de·*lan*·te de ...
next to ...	al lado de ... al *la*·do de ...
opposite ...	frente a ... *fren*·te a ...
straight ahead	todo derecho *to*·do de·*re*·cho

Airport & Transport

≡ Fast Phrases

When's the next (bus)?	¿A qué hora es el próximo (autobús)? a ke o·ra es el *prok*·see·mo (ow·to·*boos*)
Does this (train) stop at ...?	¿Para el (tren) en ...? *pa*·ra el (tren) en ...
One ticket to ..., please.	Un boleto a ..., por favor. oon bo·*le*·to a ... por fa·*vor*

At the Airport

I'm here on business.	Estoy aquí de negocios. es·*toy* a·kee de ne·*go*·syos
I'm here on holiday.	Estoy aquí de vacaciones. es·*toy* a·kee de va·ka·*syo*·nes
I'm here for (three) days.	Estoy aquí por (tres) días. es·*toy* a·kee por (tres) *dee*·as
I'm here for (two) weeks.	Estoy aquí por (dos) semanas. es·*toy* a·kee por (dos) se·*ma*·nas
I'm here in transit.	Estoy aquí en tránsito. es·*toy* a·kee en *tran*·see·to

24

I'm going to ...	Voy a ... voy a ...
I have nothing to declare.	No tengo nada que declarar. no ten·go na·da ke de·kla·rar
I have something to declare.	Tengo algo que declarar. ten·go al·go ke de·kla·rar

Getting Around

PHRASE BUILDER

At what time does the ... leave?	¿A qué hora sale ...?	a ke o·ra sa·le ...
boat	el barco	el bar·ko
bus (city)	el autobús; la chiva (Col); el colectivo (Arg); la guagua (Cub); el micro (Bol, Chi)	el ow·to·boos; la chee·va; el ko·lek·tee·vo; la gwa·gwa; el mee·kro
bus (intercity)	el ómnibus; el micro (Arg)	el om·nee·boos; el mee·kro
plane	el avión	el a·vyon
train	el tren	el tren

When's the first bus?	¿A qué hora es el primer autobús? a ke o·ra es el pree·mer ow·to·boos
When's the last bus?	¿A qué hora es el último autobús? a ke o·ra es el ool·tee·mo ow·to·boos
How long does the trip take?	¿Cuánto se tarda? kwan·to se tar·da

25

Is it a direct route?	¿Es un viaje directo? es oon *vya*·khe dee·*rek*·to
That's my seat.	Ése es mi asiento. e·se es mee a·*syen*·to
Is this seat free?	¿Está libre este asiento? es·*ta* lee·bre es·te a·*syen*·to
✂ Is it free?	¿Está libre? es·*ta* lee·bre

Buying Tickets

Where can I buy a ticket?	¿Dónde puedo comprar un boleto? don·de pwe·do kom·*prar* oon bo·*le*·to
Do I need to book?	¿Tengo que reservar? *ten*·go ke re·ser·*var*
What time do I have to check in?	¿A qué hora tengo que facturar mi equipaje? a ke o·ra *ten*·go ke fak·too·*rar* mee e·kee·*pa*·khe

PHRASE BUILDER

One ... ticket to (Lima), please.	Un boleto ... a (Lima), por favor.	oon bo·*le*·to ... a (*lee*·ma) por fa·*vor*
1st-class	de primera clase	de pree·*me*·ra *kla*·se
2nd-class	de segunda clase	de se·*goon*·da *kla*·se
child's	infantil	een·fan·*teel*
return	de ida y vuelta	de *ee*·da ee *vwel*·ta
student's	de estudiante	de es·too·*dyan*·te

I'd like an aisle seat.	Quisiéra un asiento de pasillo.
	kee·*sye*·ra oon a·*syen*·to de pa·*see*·yo
I'd like a window seat.	Quisiéra un asiento junto a la ventana.
	kee·*sye*·ra oon a·*syen*·to *khoon*·to a la ven·*ta*·na
I'd like a (non)smoking seat.	Quisiéra un asiento de (no) fumadores.
	kee·*sye*·ra oon a·*syen*·to de (no) foo·ma·*do*·res

Luggage

My luggage has been damaged.	Mi equipaje ha sido dañado.
	mee e·kee·*pa*·khe a *see*·do da·*nya*·do
My luggage has been lost.	Mi equipaje ha sido perdido.
	mee e·kee·*pa*·khe a *see*·do per·*dee*·do
My luggage has been stolen.	Mi equipaje ha sido robado.
	mee e·kee·*pa*·khe a *see*·do ro·*ba*·do
I'd like a luggage locker.	Quisiera un casillero de consigna.
	kee·*sye*·ra oon ka·see·*ye*·ro de kon·*seeg*·na
I'd like some coins/tokens.	Quisiera unas monedas/fichas.
	kee·*sye*·ra *oo*·nas mo·*ne*·das/*fee*·chas

Bus & Train

Where's the bus stop?	¿Dónde está la parada del autobús? *don·*de es·*ta* la pa·*ra·*da del ow·to·*boos*
Which bus goes to (the centre of town)?	¿Qué autobús va al (centro de la cuidad)? ke ow·to·*boos* va al (*sen·*tro de la syoo·*da*)
Is this the bus to ...?	¿Es el ómnibus para ...? es el *om·*nee·boos *pa·*ra ...
What station is this?	¿Cuál es esta estación? kwal es *es·*ta es·ta·*syon*
What's the next station?	¿Cuál es la próxima estación? kwal es la *prok·*see·ma es·ta·*syon*
Does this train stop at ...?	¿Para el tren en ...? *pa·*ra el tren en ...
Do I need to change trains?	¿Tengo que cambiar de tren? *ten·*go ke kam·*byar* de tren
How many stops to (the museum)?	¿Cuantas paradas hay hasta (el museo)? *kwan·*tas pa·*ra·*das ai *as·*ta (el moo·*se·*o)
Do you stop at (the market)?	¿Tiene parada en (el mercado)? *tye·*ne pa·*ra·*da en (el mer·*ka·*do)
Can you tell me when we get to ...?	¿Me puede decir cuándo lleguemos a ...? me *pwe·*de de·*seer* kwan·do ye·*ge·*mos a ...

| I want to get off here. | Quiero bajarme aquí. |
| | *kye*·ro ba·*khar*·me a·*kee* |

Taxi

Where's the taxi stand?	¿Dónde está la parada de taxis?
	don·de es·*ta* la pa·*ra*·da de *tak*·sees
I'd like a taxi at (9am).	Quisiera un taxi a las (nueve de la mañana).
	kee·*sye*·ra oon taxi a las (*nwe*·ve de la ma·*nya*·na)
Is this taxi free?	¿Está libre este taxi?
	es·*ta lee*·bre *es*·te *tak*·see
✂ Is it free?	¿Está libre?
	es·*ta lee*·bre
How much is it (to the airport)?	¿Cuánto cuesta ir (al aeropuerto)?
	kwan·to *kwes*·ta eer (al a·e·ro·*pwer*·to)
Please put the meter on.	Por favor, ponga el taxímetro.
	por fa·*vor pon*·ga el tak·*see*·me·tro
Please take me to (this address).	Por favor, lléveme a (esta dirección).
	por fa·*vor ye*·ve·me a (*es*·ta dee·rek·*syon*)
✂ To ...	A ...
	a ...
Please slow down.	Por favor vaya más despacio.
	por fa·*vor va*·ya mas des·*pa*·syo

Please wait here.	Por favor espere aquí.
	por fa·*vor* es·*pe*·re a·*kee*
Stop at the corner.	Pare en la esquina.
	pa·re en la es·*kee*·na
Stop here.	Pare aquí.
	pa·re a·*kee*

Car & Motorbike

I'd like to hire a car.	Quisiera alquilar un carro.
	kee·*sye*·ra al·kee·*lar* oon *ka*·ro
	Quisiera alquilar un auto. **(SAm)**
	kee·*sye*·ra al·kee·*lar* oon *ow*·to
I'd like to hire a motorbike.	Quisiera alquilar una moto.
	kee·*sye*·ra al·kee·*lar* oo·na *mo*·to
How much for daily hire?	¿Cuánto cuesta alquilar por día?
	kwan·to *kwes*·ta al·kee·*lar* por *dee*·a
How much for weekly hire?	¿Cuánto cuesta alquilar por semana?
	kwan·to *kwes*·ta al·kee·*lar* por se·*ma*·na
Is this the road to ...?	¿Se va a ... por esta carretera?
	se va a ... por *es*·ta ka·re·*te*·ra
(How long) Can I park here?	¿(Por cuánto tiempo) Puedo aparcar aquí?
	(por *kwan*·to *tyem*·po) *pwe*·do a·par·*kar* a·*kee*
Where's a petrol station?	¿Dónde hay una gasolinera?
	don·de ai oo·na ga·so·lee·*ne*·ra

Fast Talk — Asking Questions

When asking a question in Spanish, simply make a statement, but raise your intonation towards the end of the sentence, as you would in English. Question words for more specific questions go at the start of the sentence: *cómo* ko·mo (how), *qué* ke (what), *cuándo* kwan·do (when), *dónde* don·de (where), *quién* kyen (who) or *por qué* por ke (why).

I need a mechanic.	Necesito un mecánico. ne·se·*see*·to oon me·*ka*·nee·ko
I had an accident.	Tuve un accidente. *too*·ve oon ak·see·*den*·te

Cycling

Can we get there by bike?	¿Podemos llegar allí en bicicleta? po·*de*·mos ye·*gar* a·*yee* en bee·see·*kle*·ta
Where can I hire a bicycle?	¿Dónde se puede alquilar una bicicleta? don·de se *pwe*·de al·kee·*lar* oo·na bee·see·*kle*·ta
Are there cycling paths?	¿Hay caminos de bici? ai ka·*mee*·nos de *bee*·see
Is there bicycle parking?	¿Hay aparcamiento de bici? ai a·par·ka·*myen*·to de *bee*·see
I have a puncture.	Se me pinchó una rueda. se me peen·*cho* oo·na *rwe*·da

Accommodation

≡ Fast Phrases

I have a reservation.	Tengo una reserva. *ten·go oo·na re·ser·va*
When/Where is breakfast served?	¿Cuándo/Dónde se sirve el desayuno? *kwan·do/don·de se seer·ve el de·sa·yoo·no*
What time is checkout?	¿A qué hora hay que dejar libre la habitación? *a ke o·ra ai ke de·khar lee·bre la a·bee·ta·syon*

Finding Accommodation

PHRASE BUILDER

Where's a ...?	¿Dónde hay ...?	*don·de ai ...*
bed and breakfast	una pensión con desayuno	*oo·na pen·syon kon de·sa·yoo·no*
guesthouse	una casa de huéspedes; una hostería (Arg, Chi)	*oo·na ka·sa de wes·pe·des; oo·na os·te·ree·a*
hotel	un hotel	*oon o·tel*
youth hostel	un albergue juvenil	*oon al·ber·ge khoo·ve·neel*

Booking & Checking In

I have a reservation.	Tengo una reserva. *ten·go oo·na re·ser·va*
Do you have a single room?	¿Tiene una habitación individual? *tye·ne oo·na a·bee·ta·syon een·dee·vee·dwal*
Do you have a double room?	¿Tiene una habitación doble? *tye·ne oo·na a·bee·ta·syon do·ble*
Do you have a twin room?	¿Tiene una habitación con dos camas? *tye·ne oo·na a·bee·ta·syon kon dos ka·mas*
✂ Are there rooms?	¿Hay cuartos disponibles? *ai kwar·tos dis·po·nee·bles*
How much is it per night?	¿Cuánto cuesta por noche? *kwan·to kwes·ta por no·che*
How much is it per person?	¿Cuánto cuesta por persona? *kwan·to kwes·ta por per·so·na*
How much is it per week?	¿Cuánto cuesta por semana? *kwan·to kwes·ta por se·ma·na*
For (three) nights/weeks.	Para (tres) noches/semanas. *pa·ra (tres) no·ches/se·ma·nas*
From (July 2) to (July 6).	Desde (el dos de julio) hasta (el seis de julio). *des·de (el dos de khool·yo) as·ta (el says de khool·yo)*
Can I see it?	¿Puedo verla? *pwe·do ver·la*

Hotels

Can you recommend somewhere cheap?	¿Puede recomendar algún sitio barato? *pwe·de re·ko·men·dar al·goon see·tyo ba·ra·to*
Can you recommend somewhere nearby?	¿Puede recomendar algún sitio cercano? *pwe·de re·ko·men·dar al·goon see·tyo ser·ka·no*
Can you recommend somewhere romantic?	¿Puede recomendar algún sitio romántico? *pwe·de re·ko·men·dar al·goon see·tyo ro·man·tee·ko*

Is breakfast included?	¿El desayuno está incluído? *el de·sa·yoo·no es·ta een·kloo·ee·do*
It's fine, I'll take it.	OK, la alquilo. *o·kay la al·kee·lo*
Do I need to pay upfront?	¿Necesito pagar por adelantado? *ne·se·see·to pa·gar por a·de·lan·ta·do*

Requests & Questions

When/Where is breakfast served?	¿Cuándo/Dónde se sirve el desayuno? *kwan·do/don·de se seer·ve el de·sa·yoo·no*

Please wake me at (seven).	Por favor, despiérteme a (las siete). por fa·*vor* des·*pyer*·te·me a (las *sye*·te)
Can I have my key, please?	¿Me puede dar la llave, por favor? me *pwe*·de dar la *ya*·ve por fa·*vor*
Can I use the kitchen?	¿Puedo usar la cocina? *pwe*·do oo·*sar* la ko·*see*·na
Can I use the telephone?	¿Puedo usar el teléfono? *pwe*·do oo·*sar* el te·*le*·fo·no
Can I use the internet?	¿Puedo usar el Internet? *pwe*·do oo·*sar* el *een*·ter·net
Do you have an elevator?	¿Hay ascensor? ai a·sen·*sor*
Do you have a laundry service?	¿Hay servicio de lavandería? ai ser·*vee*·syo de la·van·de·*ree*·a
Do you have a safe?	¿Hay una caja fuerte? ai *oo*·na *ka*·kha *fwer*·te
Can I get another ...?	¿Puede darme otro/a ...? m/f *pwe*·de *dar*·me o·*tro*/a ...
Do you change money here?	¿Aquí cambian dinero? a·*kee* *kam*·byan dee·*ne*·ro
Do you arrange tours here?	¿Aquí organizan paseos guiados? a·*kee* or·ga·*nee*·san pa·*se*·os gee·*a*·dos
Can I leave a message for someone?	¿Puedo dejar un mensaje para alguien? *pwe*·do de·*khar* oon men·*sa*·khe *pa*·ra al·gyen

Complaints

There's no hot water.	No hay agua caliente.	no ai *a*·gwa kal·*yen*·te

PHRASE BUILDER

The ... doesn't work.	No funciona ...	no foon·*syo*·na ...
air-conditioning	el aire acondicionado	el *ai*·re a·kon·dee·syo·*na*·do
heater	la estufa	la es·*too*·fa
toilet	el baño	el *ba*·nyo
window	la ventana	la ven·*ta*·na

The room is too dark.	La habitación es demasiado oscura.	la a·bee·ta·*syon* es de·ma·sya·do os·*koo*·ra
The room is too noisy.	La habitación es demasiado ruidosa.	la a·bee·ta·*syon* es de·ma·sya·do rwee·*do*·sa
The room is too small.	La habitación es demasiado pequeña.	la a·bee·ta·*syon* es de·ma·sya·do pe·*ke*·nya

PHRASE BUILDER

Can I get another ...?	¿Puede darme otra ...?	*pwe*·de *dar*·me *o*·tra ...
blanket	frazada	fra·*sa*·da
pillow	almohada	al·mo·*a*·da
sheet	sábana	*sa*·ba·na
towel	toalla	to·*a*·ya

ACCOMMODATION

Fast Talk Using Patterns

Look out for patterns of words or phrases that stay the same, even when the situation changes, eg 'Do you have ...?' or 'I'd like to ...' (see p8). If you can recognise these patterns, you're already halfway to creating a full phrase. The dictionary will help you put other words together with these patterns to convey your meaning – even if it's not completely grammatically correct in all contexts, the dictionary form will always be understood.

Checking Out

What time is checkout?	¿A qué hora hay que dejar libre la habitación? a ke o·ra ai ke de·khar lee·bre la a·bee·ta·syon
Can I leave my luggage here until (tonight)?	¿Puedo dejar el equipaje aquí hasta (esta noche)? pwe·do de·khar el e·kee·pa·khe a·kee as·ta (es·ta no·che)
Can I have my deposit, please?	¿Me puede dar mi depósito, por favor? me pwe·de dar mee de·po·see·to por fa·vor
Can I have my valuables, please?	¿Me puede dar mis objetos de valor, por favor? me pwe·de dar mees ob·khe·tos de va·lor por fa·vor
I had a great stay, thank you.	Tuve una estancia muy agradable, gracias. too·ve oo·na es·tan·sya mooy a·gra·da·ble gra·syas

Eating & Drinking

≡ Fast Phrases

Can I see the menu, please?	¿Puedo ver el menú, por favor?
	pwe·do ver el me·*noo* por fa·*vor*
I'd like (a beer), please.	Quisiera (una cerveza), por favor.
	kee·*sye*·ra (*oo*·na ser·*ve*·sa) por fa·*vor*
Please bring the bill.	Por favor me trae la cuenta.
	por fa·*vor* me *tra*·e la *kwen*·ta

Meals

breakfast	desayuno m
	de·sa·*yoo*·no
lunch	comida f
	ko·*mee*·da
dinner	cena f
	se·na
eat/drink	comer/beber
	ko·*mer*/be·*ber*

Finding a Place to Eat

Can you recommend a bar?	¿Puede recomendar un bar? *pwe*·de re·ko·men·*dar* oon bar
Can you recommend a cafe?	¿Puede recomendar una cafetería? *pwe*·de re·ko·men·*dar* oo·na ka·fe·te·*ree*·a
Can you recommend a restaurant?	¿Puede recomendar un restaurante? *pwe*·de re·ko·men·*dar* oon res·tow·*ran*·te
I'd like to reserve a table for (eight) o'clock.	Quisiera reservar una mesa para las (ocho). kee·*sye*·ra re·ser·*var* oo·na *me*·sa *pa*·ra las (*o*·cho)
I'd like to reserve a table for (two) people.	Quisiera reservar una mesa para (dos) personas. kee·*sye*·ra re·ser·*var* oo·na *me*·sa *pa*·ra (dos) per·*so*·nas
✂ **For two, please.**	Para dos, por favor. *pa*·ra dos por fa·*vor*
I'd like a (non)smoking table, please.	Quisiera una mesa de (no) fumadores, por favor. kee·*sye*·ra oo·na *me*·sa de (no) foo·ma·*do*·res por fa·*vor*
Are you still serving food?	¿Siguen sirviendo comida? *see*·gen seer·*vyen*·do ko·*mee*·da
How long is the wait?	¿Cuánto hay que esperar? *kwan*·to ai ke es·pe·*rar*

Ordering & Paying

Can I see the menu, please?	¿Puedo ver el menú, por favor?	
	pwe·do ver el me·*noo* por fa·*vor*	
✂ Menu, please.	El menú, por favor.	
	el me·*noo* por fa·*vor*	
What would you recommend?	¿Qué me recomienda?	
	ke me re·ko·*myen*·da	
I'd like a local speciality.	Quisiera un plato típico.	
	kee·*sye*·ra oon *pla*·to *tee*·pee·ko	
I'll have that dish, please.	Quisiera ese plato.	
	kee·*sye*·ra e·se *pla*·to	
I'd like the drink list, please.	Quisiera la lista de bebidas, por favor.	
	kee·*sye*·ra la *lees*·ta de be·*bee*·das por fa·*vor*	

Local Knowledge — Restaurants

Where would you go for a celebration?	¿Adónde se va para festejar?
	a·*don*·de se va *pa*·ra fes·te·*khar*
Where would you go for a cheap meal?	¿Adónde se va para comer una comida barata?
	a·*don*·de se va *pa*·ra ko·*mer* oo·na ko·*mee*·da ba·*ra*·ta
Where would you go for local specialities?	¿Adónde se va para comer comida típica?
	a·*don*·de se va *pa*·ra ko·*mer* ko·*mee*·da *tee*·pee·ka

PHRASE BUILDER

I'd like it ...	Lo quisiera ...	lo kee·*sye*·ra ...
medium	no muy hecho	no mooy e·cho
rare	vuelta y vuelta	*vwel*·ta ee *vwel*·ta
steamed	al vapor	al va·*por*
well-done	muy hecho	mooy e·cho
with (the dressing on the side)	con (el aliño aparte)	kon (el a·*lee*·nyo a·*par*·te)
without ...	sin ...	seen ...

Please bring (a glass).	Por favor nos trae (un vaso). por fa·*vor* nos *tra*·e (oon va·so)
Is there any (tomato sauce)?	¿Hay (salsa de tomate)? ai (*sal*·sa de to·*ma*·te)
I didn't order this.	Yo no he pedido esto. yo no e pe·*dee*·do es·to
This is (too) cold.	Esto está (demasiado) frío. es·to es·*ta* (de·ma·*sya*·do) *free*·o
This is burnt.	Esto está quemado. es·to es·*ta* ke·*ma*·do
That was delicious!	¡Estaba buenísimo! es·*ta*·ba bwe·*nee*·see·mo
Please bring the bill.	Por favor me trae la cuenta. por fa·*vor* me *tra*·e la *kwen*·ta
✂ **Bill, please.**	La cuenta, por favor. la *kwen*·ta por fa·*vor*
There's a mistake in the bill.	Hay un error en la cuenta. ai oon e·*ror* en la *kwen*·ta

41

Special Diets & Allergies

Is there a vegetarian restaurant near here?	¿Hay un restaurante vegetariano por aquí? ai oon res·tow·*ran*·te ve·khe·ta·*rya*·no por a·*kee*
Do you have vegetarian food?	¿Tienen comida vegetariana? *tye*·nen ko·*mee*·da ve·khe·ta·*rya*·na
I'm a vegetarian.	Soy vegetariano/a. **m/f** soy ve·khe·ta·*rya*·no/a
I'm a vegan.	Soy vegetariano/a estricto/a. **m/f** soy ve·khe·ta·*rya*·no/a es·*treek*·to/a
I don't eat (red meat).	No como (carne roja). no *ko*·mo (*kar*·ne *ro*·kha)
Could you prepare a meal without butter?	¿Me puede preparar una comida sin mantequilla? me *pwe*·de pre·pa·*rar* oo·na ko·*mee*·da seen man·te·*kee*·ya
Could you prepare a meal without eggs?	¿Me puede preparar una comida sin huevos? me *pwe*·de pre·pa·*rar* oo·na ko·*mee*·da seen *we*·vos

Fast Talk · Practising Spanish

If you want to practise your language skills, try the waiters at a restaurant. Find your feet with straight-forward phrases such as asking for a table and ordering a drink, then initiate a conversation by asking for menu recommendations or asking how a dish is cooked. And as you'll often know food terms even before you've 'officially' learnt a word of the language, you're already halfway to understanding the response.

Could you prepare a meal without meat stock?	¿Me puede preparar una comida sin caldo de carne? me *pwe*·de pre·pa·*rar* oo·na ko·*mee*·da seen *kal*·do de *kar*·ne

PHRASE BUILDER

I'm allergic to ...	Soy alérgico/a ... m/f	soy a·*ler*·khee·ko/a ...
dairy produce	a los productos lácteos	a los pro·*dook*·tos *lak*·te·os
fish	al pescado	al pes·*ka*·do
gluten	al gluten	al *gloo*·ten
MSG	al glutamato monosódico	al gloo·ta·*ma*·to mo·no·so·*dee*·ko
nuts	a las nueces	a las *nwe*·ses
peanuts	al maní	al ma·*nee*
pork	al cerdo	al *ser*·do
poultry	a las aves	a las *a*·ves
seafood	al marisco	al ma·*rees*·ko

Nonalcoholic Drinks

coffee (without sugar)	café m (sin azúcar) ka·*fe* (seen a·*soo*·kar)
(fruit) milkshake	licuado m (de frutas) lee·*kwa*·do (de *froo*·tas)
orange juice	jugo m de naranja *khoo*·go de na·*ran*·kha
soft drink	gaseosa f ga·se·*o*·sa

43

| tea (with milk) | té m (con leche)
te (kon *le*·che) |
| (mineral) water | agua f (mineral)
a·gwa (mee·ne·*ral*) |

Alcoholic Drinks

champagne	champán m cham·*pan*
cocktail	combinado m kom·bee·*na*·do
a shot of (whisky)	un trago de (güisqui) oon *tra*·go de (*gwees*·kee)
draught beer	cerveza f de baril ser·*ve*·sa de ba·*reel*
a glass of beer	un vaso de cerveza oon *va*·so de ser·*ve*·sa
a jug of beer	una jarra de cerveza *oo*·na *kha*·ra de ser·*ve*·sa un chop de cerveza (SAm) oon chop de ser·*ve*·sa
a pint of beer	una pinta de cerveza *oo*·na *peen*·ta de ser·*ve*·sa

---

PHRASE BUILDER

a bottle/glass of ... wine	una botella/ copa de vino ...	*oo*·na bo·*te*·ya/ *ko*·pa de *vee*·no ...
dessert	dulce	*dool*·se
red	tinto	*teen*·to
rose	rosado	ro·*sa*·do
sparkling	espumoso	es·poo·*mo*·so
white	blanco	*blan*·ko

Fast Talk Diminutives

Spanish is rich in diminutives, which are formed by adding endings such as *-ito/a* ·*ee*·to/a, *-cito/a* ·*see*·to/a, *-ico/a* ·*ee*·ko/a and *-cillo/a* ·*see*·lyo/a to words. They're often used to indicate the smallness of something or that a speaker finds something charming. This gives a friendly tone to a conversation – *un momentito* oon mo·men·*tee*·to (just a moment) sounds more light-hearted than *un momento* oon mo·*men*·to.

In the Bar

I'll buy you a drink.	Te invito a una copa. te een·*vee*·to a *oo*·na *ko*·pa
What would you like?	¿Qué quieres tomar? ke *kye*·res to·*mar*
I'd like (a beer), please.	Quisiera (una cerveza), por favor. kee·*sye*·ra (*oo*·na ser·*ve*·sa) por fa·*vor*
Same again, please.	Otra de lo mismo. o·tra de lo *mees*·mo
It's my round.	Es mi ronda. es mee *ron*·da
Cheers!	¡Salud! sa·*loo*

Buying Food

How much is (a kilo of cheese)?	¿Cuánto vale (un kilo de queso)? *kwan*·to *va*·le (oon *kee*·lo de *ke*·so)

45

Do you have anything cheaper?	¿Tiene algo más barato? *tye*·ne *al*·go mas ba·*ra*·to
What's that?	¿Qué es eso? ke es e·so
Can I taste it?	¿Puedo probarlo/a? **m/f** *pwe*·do pro·*bar*·lo/a
Do you have other kinds?	¿Tiene otros tipos? *tye*·ne *ot*·ros *tee*·pos
Do you sell locally produced food?	¿Vende productos locales? *ven*·de pro·*dook*·tos lo·*ka*·les

PHRASE BUILDER

I'd like ...	Déme ...	*de*·me ...
(200) grams	(doscientos) gramos	(do·*syen*·tos) *gra*·mos
(two) kilos	(dos) kilos	(dos) *kee*·los
(three) pieces	(tres) trozos	(tres) *tro*·sos
(six) slices	(seis) lonchas	(says) *lon*·chas
some ...	unos ... **m pl** unas ... **f pl**	*oo*·nos ... *oo*·nas ...
that one	ése/ésa **m/f**	e·se/e·sa
this one	éste/ésta **m/f**	e·ste/e·sta

Less.	Menos. *me*·nos
Enough.	Ya. ya
A bit more.	Un poco más. oon *po*·ko mas

Menu Decoder

This miniguide to Latin American cuisine is designed to help you navigate menus. Spanish nouns have their gender indicated by ⓜ or ⓕ. If it's a plural noun, you'll also see pl.

- a -

a la plancha a la *plan*·cha grilled
abrebocas ⓕ pl a·bre·*bo*·kas appetisers
aceitunas ⓕ pl a·say·*too*·nas olives
achicoria ⓕ a·chee·*ko*·rya chicory • endive
achuras ⓕ pl a·*choo*·ras offal
aguacate ⓜ a·gwa·*ka*·te avocado
ahumado/a ⓜ/ⓕ a·oo·*ma*·do/a smoked
ají ⓜ a·*khee* red chilli • chilli sauce
ajiaco ⓜ a·*khya*·ko spicy potato stew
ajo ⓜ a·*kho* garlic
ajoporro ⓜ a·kho·*po*·ro leek
al ajillo al a·*khee*·yo in garlic
al horno al *or*·no baked
al vapor al va·*por* steamed
albahaca ⓕ al·*ba*·ka basil
albóndigas ⓕ pl al·*bon*·dee·gas meatballs
alcachofa ⓕ al·ka·*cho*·fa artichoke
alcaparra ⓕ al·ka·*pa*·ra caper
alioli ⓜ a·*yo*·lee garlic sauce
almejas ⓕ pl al·*me*·khas clams
almendra ⓕ al·*men*·dra almond
alubias ⓕ pl a·*loo*·byas kidney beans
ananá(s) ⓜ a·na·*na(s)* pineapple
anchoas ⓕ pl an·*cho*·as anchovies
anguila ⓕ an·*gee*·la eel

anís ⓜ a·*nees* anise • aniseed
aperitivos ⓜ pl a·pe·ree·*tee*·vos aperitifs
apio ⓜ *a*·pyo celery
arenque ⓜ a·*ren*·ke herring
arrollado ⓜ a·ro·*ya*·do rolled pork
arroz ⓜ a·*ros* rice
arvejas ⓕ pl ar·*ve*·khas peas
asado ⓜ a·*sa*·do mixed grill
asado/a ⓜ/ⓕ a·*sa*·do/a roasted
atún ⓜ a·*toon* tuna
ave ⓜ *a*·ve fowl • poultry
avellana ⓕ a·ve·*ya*·na hazelnut
azafran ⓜ a·sa·*fran* saffron

- b -

bacalao ⓜ ba·ka·*la*·o (salted) cod
batata ⓕ ba·*ta*·ta sweet potato
bebida ⓕ be·*bee*·da drink (beverage)
beicon ⓜ bay·*kon* bacon
berberechos ⓜ pl ber·be·*re*·chos cockles
berenjena ⓕ be·ren·*khe*·na eggplant • aubergine
berro ⓜ *be*·ro watercress
besugo ⓜ be·*soo*·go bream
bien asado/a ⓜ/ⓕ byen a·*sa*·do/a well-done
bien hecho/a ⓜ/ⓕ byen e·*cho*/a well-done
bistec ⓜ bees·*tek* steak

47

bollos ⓜ pl *bo·*yos bread rolls
breva ⓕ *bre·*va fig
buey ⓜ bway ox

~ c ~

caballa ⓕ ka·*ba·*ya mackerel
cabra ⓕ *ka·*bra goat
calabacín ⓜ ka·la·ba·*seen* zucchini •
courgette
calabaza ⓕ ka·la·*ba·*sa pumpkin •
gourd • marrow
calamares ⓜ pl ka·la·*ma·*res
calamari • squid
caldereta ⓕ kal·de·*re·*ta stew
caldo ⓜ *kal·*do broth • stock
camarón ⓜ ka·ma·*ron* shrimp •
small prawn
camote ⓜ ka·*mo·*te sweet potato
canela ⓕ ka·*ne·*la cinnamon
canelones ⓜ pl ka·ne·*lo·*nes
cannelloni
cangrejo ⓜ kan·*gre·*kho crab
capón ⓜ ka·*pon* mutton
carabinero ⓜ ka·ra·bee·*ne·*ro large
prawn
caracol ⓜ ka·ra·*kol* snail
carne ⓕ *kar·*ne meat
carpa ⓕ *kar·*pa carp
castaña ⓕ kas·*ta·*nya chestnut
caza ⓕ *ka·*sa game (meat)
cazuela ⓕ ka·*swe·*la casserole •
fish stew
cebada ⓕ se·*ba·*da barley
cebolla ⓕ se·*bo·*ya onion
cerdo ⓜ *ser·*do pig • pork
cereza ⓕ se·*re·*sa cherry
cerveza ⓕ ser·*ve·*sa beer
ceviche ⓜ se·*vee·*che marinated
raw fish
chalote ⓜ cha·*lo·*te spring onion •
shallot
champiñones ⓜ pl
cham·pee·*nyo·*nes mushrooms
chauchas ⓕ pl *chow·*chas string

beans
chicharrón ⓜ chee·cha·*ron* fried
pork fat
chile ⓜ *chee·*le small red pepper
chinchulines ⓜ pl
cheen·choo·*lee·*nes small intestines
chipirón ⓜ chee·pee·*ron* small squid
chirimoya ⓕ chee·ree·*mo·*ya custard
apple
chivo ⓜ *chee·*vo kid • baby goat
choclo ⓜ *cho·*klo maize • corn on
the cob
choco ⓜ *cho·*ko cuttlefish
chop ⓜ chop draught beer
chorizo ⓜ cho·*ree·*so spicy pork
sausage
chuleta ⓕ choo·*le·*ta chop • cutlet
chupe ⓜ *choo·*pe stew • soup
churrasco ⓜ choo·*ras·*ko rib steak
ciruela ⓕ see·*rwe·*la plum
cocinado/a ⓜ/ⓕ ko·see·*na·*do/a
cooked
coco ⓜ *ko·*ko coconut
codorniz ⓕ ko·dor·*nees* quail
coliflor ⓕ ko·lee·*flor* cauliflower
combinado ⓜ kom·bee·*na·*do
cocktail
coñac ⓜ ko·*nyak* brandy
conejo ⓜ ko·*ne·*kho rabbit
cordero ⓜ kor·*de·*ro lamb
costillar ⓜ **de cordero** kos·tee·*yar*
de kor·*de·*ro rack of lamb
crudo/a ⓜ/ⓕ *kroo·*do/a raw
crustáceos ⓜ pl kroos·*ta·*se·os
shellfish
cuadril ⓜ *kwa·*dreel rump steak
cuy ⓜ kooy grilled or roasted guinea
pig

~ d ~

damasco ⓜ da·*mas·*ko apricot
dátil ⓜ *da·*teel date
de entrada de en·*tra·*da starters
digestivos ⓜ pl dee·khes·*tee·*vos

48

digestifs

dorado/a ⓜ/ⓕ do·*ra*·do/a browned

dulces ⓜ pl *dool*·ses confectionery • sweets

~ e ~

elote e·*lo*·te corn • corn on the cob

empanada ⓕ em·pa·*na*·da stuffed meat & vegetable turnover

enchilladas ⓕ pl en·chee·*ya*·das crisp fried tortilla topped with spicy meat, salad & crumbled cheese

eneldo ⓜ e·*nel*·do dill

ensalada ⓕ en·sa·*la*·da salad

entremeses ⓕ pl en·tre·*me*·ses hors-d'oeuvres

espagueti ⓜ es·pa·*ge*·tee spaghetti

espárragos ⓜ pl es·*pa*·ra·gos asparagus

espinacas ⓜ pl es·pee·*na*·kas spinach

estofado ⓜ es·to·*fa*·do stew

estofado/a ⓜ/ⓕ es·to·*fa*·do/a braised

estragón ⓜ es·tra·*gon* tarragon

~ f ~

faba ⓜ *fa*·ba type of dried bean

faisán ⓜ fai·*san* pheasant

fideos ⓜ pl fee·*de*·os noodles

filete ⓜ fee·*le*·te fillet of meat or fish

flan ⓜ flan egg custard • creme caramel

frambuesa ⓕ fram·*bwe*·sa raspberry

fresa ⓕ *fre*·sa strawberry

frescos ⓜ pl *fres*·kos fruit drinks blended with water & sugar

frijoles ⓜ pl free·*kho*·les beans

fritada ⓕ free·*ta*·da scraps of fried or roast pork

fritanga ⓕ free·*tan*·ga hotpot or stew

frito/a ⓜ/ⓕ *free*·to/a fried

fruta ⓕ *froo*·ta fruit

frutilla ⓕ froo·*tee*·ya strawberry

~ g ~

galleta ⓕ ga·*ye*·ta biscuit • cookie

gallina ⓕ ga·*yee*·na chicken

gallito ⓜ ga·*yee*·to cockerel

gallo ⓜ *ga*·yo rooster

gambas ⓕ pl **rebozadas** gam·bas rebo·sa·das batter-fried large prawns

ganso ⓜ *gan*·so goose

garbanzo ⓜ gar·*ban*·so chickpea

gazpacho ⓜ ga·*spa*·cho cold tomato & vegetable soup

girasol ⓜ khee·ra·*sol* sunflower

granada ⓕ gra·*na*·da pomegranate

gratinado/a ⓜ/ⓕ gra·tee·*na*·do/a au gratin

grosella ⓕ gro·*se*·ya redcurrant

guindilla ⓕ geen·*dee*·ya hot chilli

guisantes ⓜ pl gee·*san*·tes peas

~ h ~

haba ⓕ *a*·ba broad bean • Lima bean

hamburguesa ⓕ am·boor·*ge*·sa hamburger

helado ⓜ e·*la*·do ice cream

hervido/a ⓜ/ⓕ er·*vee*·do/a boiled

hierba ⓕ *yer*·ba herb

hierbabuena ⓕ yer·ba·*bwe*·na spearmint

hígado ⓜ *ee*·ga·do liver

higo ⓜ *ee*·go fig

hocico ⓜ o·*see*·ko snout

hongo ⓜ *on*·go button mushroom

horneado/a ⓜ/ⓕ or·ne·*a*·do/a baked

huevos ⓜ pl *we*·vos eggs

- i -

infusión ⓜ een·foo·*syon* herbal tea

- j -

jabalí ⓜ kha·ba·*lee* wild boar
jamón ⓜ kha·*mon* ham
jengibre ⓜ khen·*khee*·bre ginger
jugo ⓜ *khoo*·go juice • milkshake

- l -

langosta ⓕ lan·*gos*·ta spiny lobster
langostino ⓜ lan·gos·*tee*·no prawn • lobster
leche ⓕ *le*·che milk
lechón ⓜ le·*chon* suckling pig
lechuga ⓕ le·*choo*·ga lettuce
legumbre ⓕ le·*goom*·bre pulse
lenguado ⓜ len·*gwa*·do lemon sole • dab
lentejas ⓕ pl len·*te*·khas lentils
licores ⓜ pl lee·*ko*·res spirits
licuados ⓜ pl lee·*kwa*·dos milk-blended fruit drinks
lima ⓕ *lee*·ma lime
limón ⓜ *lee*·mon lemon
limonada ⓕ lee·mo·*na*·das lemonade
lomo ⓜ *lo*·mo loin
longaniza ⓕ lon·ga·*nee*·sa dark pork sausage

- m -

macarrones ⓜ pl ma·ka·*ro*·nes macaroni
maíz ⓜ ma·*ees* corn • maize • sweet corn
mandarina ⓕ man·da·*ree*·na mandarine • tangerine
maní ⓜ ma·*nee* peanut
mantequilla ⓕ man·te·*kee*·ya butter

manzana ⓕ man·*sa*·na apple
maracuyá ⓕ ma·ra·koo·*ya* passionfruit
marinado/a ⓜ/ⓕ ma·ree·*na*·do/a marinated
mariscos ⓜ pl ma·*rees*·kos seafood • shellfish
mayonesa ⓕ ma·yo·*ne*·sa mayonnaise
mazapan ⓜ ma·*sa*·pan marzipan • almond paste
mazorca ⓕ ma·*sor*·ka corn on the cob
mejillones ⓜ pl me·khee·*yo*·nes mussels
melocotón ⓜ me·lo·ko·*ton* peach
membrillo ⓜ mem·*bree*·yo quince
menta ⓕ *men*·ta mint
menudencias ⓕ pl me·noo·*den*·syas giblets
menudo de pollo me·*noo*·do de *po*·yo gizzard • poultry entrails
merluza ⓕ pl mer·*loo*·sa hake
mermelada ⓕ mer·me·*la*·da jam
miel ⓕ myel honey
migas ⓕ pl *mee*·gas fried breadcrumb dish
milanesa ⓕ mee·la·*ne*·sa schnitzel
mojama ⓕ mo·*kha*·ma cured tuna
molleja ⓕ mo·*ye*·kha sweetbread
montado ⓜ mon·*ta*·do tiny sandwich served as an appetiser
mora ⓕ *mo*·ra blackberry
morcilla ⓕ mor·*see*·ya blood sausage
mostaza ⓕ mos·*ta*·sa mustard
muslo ⓜ *moos*·lo thigh
muy hecho/a ⓜ/ⓕ mooy e·*cho*/a well-done

- n -

nabo ⓜ *na*·bo turnip
naranja ⓕ na·*ran*·kha orange
naranjadas ⓕ pl na·ran·*kha*·das lemonades made with orange juice

nata ① *na·*ta cream
natillas ① pl na·*tee·*yas custard •
creamy milk dessert
nuez ⓜ nwes nut • walnut

- o -

orejón ⓜ o·re·*khon* dried apricot
ostión ⓜ os·*tyon* scallop
ostras ① pl os·tras oysters
oveja ① o·*ve·*kha ewe

- p -

paloma ① pa·*lo·*ma pigeon
palta ① *pal·*ta avocado
pan ⓜ pan bread
papas ① pl *pa·*pas potatoes
papitas ① pl pa·*pee·*tas potato chips
parrilla ① pa·*ree·*ya grill
parrillada ① pa·ree·*ya·*da mixed grill
pasa ⓜ *pa·*sa raisin • sultana
pastel ⓜ pas·*tel* pastry • cake
patita ① **de cerdo** pa·*tee·*ta de
ser·do pig's trotter
pato ⓜ *pa·*to duck
pavo ⓜ *pa·*vo turkey
pechuga ① pe·*choo·*ga breast meat
pepinillo ⓜ pe·pee·*nee·*yo gherkin
pepino ⓜ pe·*pee·*no cucumber
pera ① *pe·*ra pear
perca ① *per·*ka perch
perdiz ① per·*dees* partridge
perejil ⓜ pe·re·*kheel* parsley
pescado ⓜ pes·*ka·*do fish
pescaíto ⓜ pes·ka·*ee·*to tiny fried fish
pez ⓜ **espada** pes es·*pa·*da
swordfish
picadillo ⓜ pee·ka·*dee·*yo minced
meat
pil pil ⓜ peel peel often spicy garlic
sauce
pimentón ⓜ pee·men·*ton* paprika
pimienta ① pee·*myen·*ta pepper
(condiment)

pimiento ⓜ pee·*myen·*to capsicum •
bell pepper
piña ① *pee·*nya pineapple
pincho ⓜ *peen·*cho kebab
piñón ⓜ pee·*nyon* pine nut
plancha ① *plan·*cha grill
plátano ⓜ *pla·*ta·no banana •
plantain
platija ① pla·*tee·*kha flounder
poché po·*che* poached
poco hecho/a ⓜ/① po·ko e·cho/a
rare
pollo ⓜ *po·*yo chicken
pomelo ⓜ po·*me·*lo grapefruit
porotos ⓜ pl po·*ro·*tos beans
porrón ⓜ **de cerveza** po·*ron* de
ser·*ve·*sa bottled beer
postre ⓜ *pos·*tre dessert
potaje ⓜ po·*ta·*khe stew
primer ⓜ **plato** pree·*mer pla·*to first
course • entree
puerros ⓜ pl *pwe·*ros leek
pulpo ⓜ *pool·*po octopus

- q -

queque ⓜ *ke·*ke cake
queso ⓜ *ke·*so cheese

- r -

rábano ⓜ *ra·*ba·no radish
ración ① ra·*syon* small tapas plate
or dish
rape ⓜ *ra·*pe monkfish
refrescos ⓜ pl re·*fres·*kos soft drinks
relleno/a ⓜ/① re·*ye·*no/a stuffed
remolacha ① re·mo·*la·*cha beetroot
repollo ⓜ re·*po·*yo cabbage
revoltijo ⓜ re·vol·*tee·*kho scrambled
egg
riñón ⓜ ree·*nyon* kidney
romero ⓜ ro·*me·*ro rosemary
rosado ⓜ ro·*sa·*do rosé
ruibarbo ⓜ *roo·*ee·bar·bo rhubarb

MENU DECODER

- s -

salchichas ① pl sal·*chee*·chas sausages similar to hot dogs
salsa ① *sal*·sa sauce
salteado/a ⓜ/① sal·te·*a*·do/a sauteed
sandía ① san·*dee*·a watermelon
sangría ① san·*gree*·a a red wine punch
seco/a ⓜ/① *se*·ko/a dry • dried
segundo ⓜ **plato** se·*goon*·do *pla*·to main course
sémola ① *se*·mo·la semolina
sepia ① *se*·pya cuttlefish
sésamo ⓜ *se*·sa·mo sesame
sidra ① *see*·dra cider
sobrasada ① so·bra·*sa*·da soft pork sausage
soja ① *so*·kha soya
solomillo ⓜ so·lo·*mee*·yo sirloin
sopa ① *so*·pa soup
suflé ⓜ soo·*fle* souffle

- t -

tallarines ⓜ pl ta·ya·*ree*·nes noodles mixed with pork, chicken, beef or vegetables
tamales ⓜ pl ta·*ma*·les cornmeal dough filled with spiced beef, vegetables & potatoes & wrapped in a maize husk & fried, grilled or baked
tarta ① *tar*·ta cake
ternera ① ter·*ne*·ra veal
tira ① **de asado** *tee*·ra de a·*sa*·do a narrow strip of rib roast

tocino ⓜ to·*see*·no bacon
tomate ⓜ to·*ma*·te tomato
torta ① *tor*·ta tart • cake • flan
tortilla ① tor·*tee*·ya omelette
tostada ① tos·*ta*·da toast
tripas ① pl *tree*·pas offal
trucha ① *troo*·cha trout
trufa ① *troo*·fa truffle
turrón ⓜ too·*ron* almond nougat

- u -

uva ① *oo*·va grape

- v -

vaca ① *va*·ka beef
vacío ⓜ va·*see*·o flank steak, textured & chewy
venado ⓜ ve·*na*·do venison
venera ① ve·*ne*·ra scallop
verduras ① pl ver·*doo*·ras green vegetables
vino ⓜ *vee*·no wine

- y -

yuca ① *yoo*·ka cassava

- z -

zanahoria ① sa·na·o·*rya* carrot
zapallo ⓜ sa·*pa*·yo pumpkin
zarzuela ① **de marisco** sar·*swe*·la de ma·*rees*·ko seafood stew

Sightseeing

Fast Phrases

When's the museum open?	¿A qué hora abre el museo? a ke *o*·ra *a*·bre el moo·*se*·o
When's the next tour?	¿A qué hora sale el próximo recorrido? a ke *o*·ra *sa*·le el *prok*·see·mo re·ko·*ree*·do
Can I take photos?	¿Puedo sacar fotos? *pwe*·do sa·*kar* fo·tos

Planning

Do you have information on local sights?	¿Tiene información sobre los lugares locales de interés? *tye*·ne een·for·ma·*syon* so·bre los loo·*ga*·res lo·*ka*·les de een·te·*res*
I have (one day).	Tengo (un día). *ten*·go (oon *dee*·a)
I'd like to see ...	Me gustaría ver ... me goos·ta·*ree*·a ver ...

| Can we hire a local guide? | ¿Podemos alquilar un guía local?
 po·*de*·mos al·kee·*lar* oon *gee*·a lo·*kal* |
| Are there guides? | ¿Hay guías?
 ai *gee*·as |

Questions

What's that?	¿Qué es eso? ke es *e*·so
How old is it?	¿De cuándo es? de *kwan*·do es
Who made it?	¿Quién lo hizo? kyen lo *ee*·so
Can I take photos (of you)?	¿(Le/Te) Puedo sacar fotos? **pol/inf** (le/te) *pwe*·do sa·*kar* *fo*·tos
Could you take a photo of me?	¿Me puede sacar una foto? me *pwe*·de sa·*kar* *oo*·na *fo*·to

---

PHRASE BUILDER

I'd like a/an ...	Quisiera ...	kee·*sye*·ra ...
audio set	un equipo audio	oon e·*kee*·po *ow*·dyo
catalogue	un catálogo	oon ka·*ta*·lo·go
guidebook (in English)	una guía turística (en inglés)	*oo*·na *gee*·a too·*rees*·tee·ka (en een·*gles*)
local map	un mapa de la zona	oon *ma*·pa de la *so*·na

Getting In

What time does it open?	¿A qué hora abre?
	a ke *o*·ra *a*·bre
What time does it close?	¿A qué hora cierra?
	a ke *o*·ra *sye*·ra
What's the admission charge?	¿Cuánto cuesta la entrada?
	kwan·to *kwes*·ta la en·*tra*·da

PHRASE BUILDER

Is there a discount for ...?	¿Hay descuentos para ...?	ai des·*kwen*·tos *pa*·ra ...
children	niños	*nee*·nyos
groups	grupos	*groo*·pos
pensioners	pensionados; jubilados (Arg)	pen·syo·*na*·dos; khoo·bee·*la*·dos
students	estudiantes	es·too·*dyan*·tes

Galleries & Museums

When's the gallery open?	¿A qué hora abre la galería?
	a ke *o*·ra *a*·bre la ga·le·*ree*·a
When's the museum open?	¿A qué hora abre el museo?
	a ke *o*·ra *a*·bre el moo·*se*·o
What's in the collection?	¿Qué hay en la colección?
	ke ai en la ko·lek·*syon*
It's an exhibition of (pottery).	Hay una exposición de (alfarería).
	ai *oo*·na ek·spo·see·*syon* de (al·fa·re·*ree*·a)
I like the works of ...	Me gusta la obra de ...
	me *goos*·ta la *o*·bra de ...

PHRASE BUILDER

... art	arte ...	*ar*·te ...
Aztec	azteca	as·*te*·ka
baroque	barroco	ba·*ro*·ko
graphic	gráfico	*gra*·fee·ko
Inca	inca	*een*·ka
Mayan	maya	*ma*·ya
modernist	modernista	mo·der·*nees*·ta
pre-Columbian	precolombino	pre·ko·lom·*bee*·no

Tours

When's the next excursion?	¿Cuándo es la próxima excursión? *kwan*·do es la *prok*·see·ma ek·skoor·*syon*
When's the next tour?	¿Cuándo es el próximo recorrido? *kwan*·do es el *prok*·see·mo re·ko·*ree*·do

Fast Talk Forming Sentences

You don't need to memorise complete sentences; instead, simply use key words to get your meaning across. For example, you might know that *cuando* *kwan*·do means 'when' in Spanish. So if you've arranged a tour but don't know what time, just ask *Recorrido cuando?* re·ko·*ree*·do *kwan*·do. Don't worry that you're not getting the whole sentence right – people will understand if you stick to the key words.

Local Knowledge Tours

Can you recommend a tour?	¿Puede recomendar algún recorrido?
	pwe·de re·ko·men·*dar* al·*goon* re·ko·*ree*·do
Can you recommend a boat trip?	¿Puede recomendar algún paseo en barca?
	pwe·de re·ko·men·*dar* al·*goon* pa·*se*·o en *bar*·ka
Can you recommend a day trip?	¿Puede recomendar alguna excursión de un día?
	pwe·de re·ko·men·*dar* al·*goo*·na ek·skoor·*syon* de oon *dee*·a

Is food included?	¿Incluye comida?
	een·*kloo*·ye ko·*mee*·da
Is transport included?	¿Incluye transporte?
	een·*kloo*·ye trans·*por*·te
Do I need to take (equipment) with me?	¿Necesito llevar (equipo)?
	ne·se·*see*·to ye·*var* (e·*kee*·po)
How long is the tour?	¿Cuánto dura el recorrido?
	kwan·to *doo*·ra el re·ko·*ree*·do
What time should I be back?	¿A qué hora tengo que volver?
	a ke *o*·ra *ten*·go ke vol·*ver*
I've lost my group.	He perdido mi grupo.
	e per·*dee*·do mee *groo*·po
I'm with them.	Voy con ellos.
	voy kon *e*·yos

Shopping

≡ Fast Phrases

Can I look at it?	¿Puedo verlo? *pwe·*do *ver·*lo
How much is it?	¿Cuánto cuesta esto? *kwan·*to *kwes·*ta *es·*to
That's too expensive.	Es muy caro. es mooy *ka·*ro

Looking For ...

Where's (a market)?	¿Dónde hay (un mercado)? *don·*de ai (oon mer·*ka·*do)
Where can I buy (locally produced goods)?	¿Dónde puedo comprar (productos locales)? *don·*de *pwe·*do kom·*prar* (pro·*dook·*tos lo·*ka·*les)

In the Shop

I'd like to buy ...	Quisiera comprar ... kee·*sye·*ra kom·*prar* ...
I'm just looking.	Sólo estoy mirando. *so·*lo es·*toy* mee·*ran·*do

Shops

Where would you go for bargains?	¿Dónde se pueden comprar productos baratos? *don*·de se *pwe*·den kom·*prar* pro·*dook*·tos ba·*ra*·tos
Where would you go for local souvenirs?	¿Dónde se pueden comprar recuerdos de esta localidad? *don*·de se *pwe*·den kom·*prar* re·*kwer*·dos de *es*·ta lo·ka·lee·*dad*

Can I look at it?	¿Puedo verlo? *pwe*·do *ver*·lo
What is this made from?	¿De qué está hecho? de ke es·*ta e*·cho
Do you have any others?	¿Tiene otros? *tye*·ne o·tros
Does it have a guarantee?	¿Tiene garantía? *tye*·ne ga·ran·*tee*·a
It's faulty.	Es defectuoso. es de·fek·*two*·so
Can I have it wrapped?	¿Me lo podría envolver? me lo po·*dree*·a en·vol·*ver*
Can I have a bag, please?	¿Podría darme una bolsa, por favor? po·*dree*·a *dar*·me *oo*·na *bol*·sa por fa·*vor*
I'd like my money back, please.	Quisiera que me devuelva el dinero, por favor. kee·*sye*·ra ke me de·*vwel*·va el dee·*ne*·ro por fa·*vor*

I'd like to return this, please.	Quisiera devolver esto, por favor.
	kee·*sye*·ra de·vol·*ver* es·to por fa·*vor*

Paying & Bargaining

How much is it?	¿Cuánto cuesta esto?
	kwan·to *kwes*·ta es·to

✂ How much?	¿Cuánto cuesta?
	kwan·to *kwes*·ta

It's (12) pesos.	Cuesta (doce) pesos.
	kwes·ta (*do*·se) *pe*·sos

Can you write down the price?	¿Puede escribir el precio?
	pwe·de es·kree·*beer* el *pre*·syo

That's too expensive.	Es muy caro.
	es mooy *ka*·ro

Do you have something cheaper?	¿Tiene algo más barato?
	tye·ne *al*·go mas ba·*ra*·to

Can you lower the price (a little)?	¿Podría bajar (un poco) el precio?
	po·*dree*·a ba·*khar* (oon *po*·ko) el *pre*·syo

I'll give you ...	Le/La daré ... **m/f pol**
	le/la da·*re* ...

Do you accept credit cards?	¿Aceptan tarjetas de crédito?
	a·*sep*·tan tar·*khe*·tas de *kre*·dee·to

I'd like my change, please.	Quisiera mi cambio, por favor.
	kee·*sye*·ra mee *kam*·byo por fa·*vor*

| Can I have a receipt, please? | ¿Podría darme un recibo, por favor? po·*dree*·a *dar*·me oon re·*see*·bo por fa·*vor* |
| | |

 Receipt, please. | Un recibo, por favor. oon re·*see*·bo por fa·*vor*

Clothes & Shoes

I'm looking for shoes.	Busco zapatos. *boos*·ko sa·*pa*·tos
I'm looking for underwear.	Busco ropa interior. *boos*·ko *ro*·pa een·te·*ryor*
My size is (medium).	Uso la talla (mediana). *oo*·so la *ta*·ya (me·*dya*·na)
Can I try it on?	¿Me lo puedo probar? me lo *pwe*·do pro·*bar*
It doesn't fit.	No me queda bien. no me *ke*·da byen

Books & Reading

Is there an English-language bookshop?	¿Hay una librería en inglés? ai *oo*·na lee·bre·*ree*·a en een·*gles*
Is there an English-language section?	¿Hay una sección en inglés? ai *oo*·na sek·*syon* en een·*gles*
Do you have a book by ...?	¿Tiene un libro de ...? *tye*·ne oon *lee*·bro de ...
I'd like a newspaper (in English).	Quisiera un periódico (en inglés). kee·*sye*·ra oon pe·*ryo*·dee·ko (en een·*gles*)

False Friends

Some Spanish words look like English words but have a different meaning altogether! For example, *suburbio* soo·*boor*·byo is 'slum district' (not 'suburb', which is *barrio* bar·yo); *injuria* een·*khoor*·ya is 'insult' (not 'injury', which is *herida* e·*ree*·da); *parientes* pa·*ryen*·tes is 'relatives' (not 'parents', which is *padres* *pad*·res); and *embarazada* em·ba·ra·*sa*·da is 'pregnant' (not 'embarassed', which is *avergonzada* a·ver·gon·*sa*·da).

I'd like a dictionary.	Quisiera un diccionario. kee·*sye*·ra oon deek·syo·*na*·ryo

Music & DVDs

I'd like a CD/DVD.	Quisiera un cómpact/DVD. kee·*sye*·ra oon *kom*·pak/ de·ve·*de*
I'd like some headphones.	Quisiera unos auriculares. kee·*sye*·ra oo·nos ow·ree·koo·*la*·res
I heard a band called ...	Escuché un grupo que se llama ... es·koo·*che* oon *groo*·po ke se *ya*·ma ...
What's their best recording?	¿Cuál es su mejor disco? kwal es soo me·*khor* dees·ko
Can I listen to this?	¿Puedo escuchar éste? *pwe*·do es·koo·*char* es·te
What region is this DVD for?	¿Para qué región es este DVD? *pa*·ra ke re·*khyon* es *es*·te de·ve·*de*

Entertainment

⇒ Fast Phrases

What's on tonight?	¿Qué hay esta noche?
	ke ai *es*·ta *no*·che
Where are the clubs?	¿Dónde hay clubs nocturnos?
	don·de ai kloobs nok·*toor*·nos
(When/Where) shall we meet?	¿(A qué hora/Dónde) quedamos?
	(a ke *o*·ra/*don*·de) ke·*da*·mos

Going Out

What's there to do in the evenings?	¿Qué se puede hacer por las noches?
	ke se *pwe*·de a·*ser* por las *no*·ches
What's on today?	¿Qué hay hoy?
	ke ai oy
What's on tonight?	¿Qué hay esta noche?
	ke ai *es*·ta *no*·che
What's on?	¿Qué hay?
	ke ai

Local Knowledge

Clubs

Can you recommend clubs?	¿Puede recomendar clubs nocturnos? *pwe·de re·ko·men·dar kloobs nok·toor·nos*
Can you recommend gay venues?	¿Puede recomendar lugares gay? *pwe·de re·ko·men·dar loo·ga·res gay*
Can you recommend pubs?	¿Puede recomendar bares? *pwe·de re·ko·men·dar ba·res*

What's on this weekend?	¿Qué hay este fin de semana? *ke ai es·te feen de se·ma·na*
Is there a local entertainment guide?	¿Hay una guía de espectáculos de la zona? *ai oo·na gee·a de es·pek·ta·koo·los de la so·na*
Is there a local gay guide?	¿Hay una guía de lugares gay? *ai oo·na gee·a de loo·ga·res gay*

PHRASE BUILDER

I feel like going to a/the ...	Tengo ganas de ir ...	*ten·go ga·nas de eer ...*
bar	a un bar	*a oon bar*
cafe	a una cafetería	*a oo·na ka·fe·te·ree·a*
movies	al cine	*al see·ne*
salsa club	a una salsoteca	*a oo·na sal·so·te·ka*
tango club	a una milonga	*a oo·na mee·lon·ga*
theatre	al teatro	*al te·a·tro*

Fast Talk

Regional Pronunciation

Pronunciation of the letters *ll* and *y* varies across Latin America. They are simplified to 'y' (as in 'yes') in much of Latin America, and drop out altogether before the vowels *e* and *i*. Be alert, though: in Argentina and Uruguay you'll hear them pronounced as the 'sh' in 'shop', in Colombia and Venezuela like the 'dg' in 'judge', and elsewhere you may hear them pronounced like the 's' in 'measure'.

Meeting Up

When shall we meet?	¿A qué hora quedamos? a ke *o*·ra ke·*da*·mos
Let's meet at (eight) o'clock.	Quedamos a las (ocho). ke·*da*·mos a las (*o*·cho)
Where will we meet?	¿Dónde quedamos? *don*·de ke·*da*·mos
Let's meet at (the entrance).	Quedamos en (la entrada). ke·*da*·mos en (la en·*tra*·da)
I'll pick you up.	Paso a recogerle. **pol** *pa*·so a re·ko·*kher*·le Paso a recogerte. **inf** *pa*·so a re·ko·*kher*·te
I'll be coming later.	Iré más tarde. ee·*re* mas *tar*·de
Where will you be?	¿Dónde estará? **pol** *don*·de es·ta·*ra* ¿Dónde estarás? **inf** *don*·de es·ta·*ras*
Sorry I'm late.	Siento llegar tarde. *syen*·to ye·*gar tar*·de

Practicalities

⩵ Fast Phrases

Where's the nearest ATM?	¿Dónde está el cajero automático más cercano? *don·de es·ta el ka·khe·ro ow·to·ma·tee·ko mas ser·ka·no*
Is there wireless internet access here?	¿Hay acceso al internet inalámbrico aquí? *ai ak·se·so al een·ter·net ee·na·lam·bree·ko a·kee*
Where are the toilets?	¿Dónde están los baños? *don·de es·tan los ba·nyos*

Banking

Where's a bank?	¿Dónde está un banco? *don·de es·ta oon ban·ko*
What time does the bank open?	¿A qué hora abre el banco? *a ke o·ra a·bre el ban·ko*
Where's the nearest ATM?	¿Dónde está el cajero automático más cercano? *don·de es·ta el ka·khe·ro ow·to·ma·tee·ko mas ser·ka·no*

Where's the nearest foreign exchange office?	¿Dónde está la oficina de cambio más cercana? *don·de es·ta la o·fee·see·na de kam·byo mas ser·ka·na*
Where can I (change money)?	¿Dónde puedo (cambiar dinero)? *don·de pwe·do (kam·byar dee·ne·ro)*
I'd like to (withdraw money).	Me gustaría (sacar dinero). *me goos·ta·ree·a (sa·kar dee·ne·ro)*
What's the exchange rate?	¿Cuál es la tasa de cambio? *kwal es la ta·sa de kam·byo*
What's the charge for that?	¿Cuánto hay que pagar por eso? *kwan·to ai ke pa·gar por e·so*

Phone/Mobile Phone

Where's the nearest public phone?	¿Dónde está la cabina telefónica más cercana? *don·de es·ta la ka·bee·na te·le·fo·nee·ka mas ser·ka·na*
I'd like to buy a phonecard.	Quiero comprar una tarjeta telefónica. *kye·ro kom·prar oo·na tar·khe·ta te·le·fo·nee·ka*
I want to make a call to (Singapore).	Quiero hacer una llamada a (Singapur). *kye·ro a·ser oo·na ya·ma·da a (seen·ga·poor)*
I want to make a reverse-charge/collect call.	Quiero hacer una llamada a cobro revertido. *kye·ro a·ser oo·na ya·ma·da a ko·bro re·ver·tee·do*

How much does a (three)-minute call cost?	¿Cuánto cuesta una llamada de (tres) minutos? *kwan·*to *kwes·*ta *oo·*na ya·*ma·*da de (tres) mee·*noo·*tos
The number is ...	El número es ... el *noo·*me·ro es ...
I've been cut off.	Me han cortado (la comunicación). me an kor·*ta·*do (la ko·moo·nee·ka·*syon*)
I'd like a charger for my phone.	Quisiera un cargador para mi teléfono. kee·*sye·*ra oon kar·ga·*dor* pa·ra mee te·*le·*fo·no
I'd like a SIM card for your network.	Quisiera una tarjeta SIM para su red. kee·*sye·*ra oo·na tar·*khe·*ta seem *pa·*ra soo re

Internet

Where's the local internet cafe?	¿Dónde hay un cibercafé cercano? *don·*de ai oon see·ber·ka·*fe* ser·*ka·*no
Is there wireless internet access here?	¿Hay acceso al internet inalámbrico aquí? ai ak·*se·*so al *een·*ter·net ee·na·*lam·*bree·ko a·*kee*
Can I connect my laptop here?	¿Se puede enchufar mi portátil aquí? se *pwe·*de en·*choo·*far mee por·*ta·*teel a·*kee*

Do you have headphones (with a microphone)?	¿Tiene audífonos (con micrófono)? *tye*·ne ow·*dee*·fo·nos (kon mee·*kro*·fo·no)

PHRASE BUILDER

I'd like to ...	Quisiera ...	kee·*sye*·ra ...
burn a CD	copiar un cómpact	ko·*pyar* oon *kom*·pak
check my email	revisar mi correo electrónico	re·vee·*sar* mee ko·*re*·o e·lek·*tro*·nee·ko
download my photos	descargar mis fotos	des·kar·*gar* mees *fo*·tos
use a printer	usar una impresora	oo·*sar* oo·na eem·pre·*so*·ra
use a scanner	usar un escáner	oo·*sar* oon es·*ka*·ner
use Skype	usar el Skype	oo·*sar* el es·*kai*·pe

How much per hour?	¿Cuánto cuesta por hora? *kwan*·to *kwes*·ta por *o*·ra
How much per page?	¿Cuánto cuesta por página? *kwan*·to *kwes*·ta por *pa*·khee·na
It's crashed.	Se ha quedado colgado. se a ke·*da*·do kol·*ga*·do
I've finished.	He terminado. e ter·mee·*na*·do
Can I connect my (camera) to this computer?	¿Puedo conectar mi (cámara) a esta computadora? *pwe*·do ko·nek·*tar* mee (*ka*·ma·ra) a es·ta kom·poo·ta·*do*·ra

Emergencies

Help!	¡Socorro! so·*ko*·ro
Stop!	¡Pare! *pa*·re
Go away!	¡Váyase! *va*·ya·se
Leave me alone!	¡Déjame en paz! *de*·kha·me en pas
Thief!	¡Ladrón! la·*dron*
Fire!	¡Fuego! *fwe*·go
Watch out!	¡Cuidado! kwee·*da*·do
Call the police!	¡Llame a la policía! *ya*·me a la po·lee·*see*·a
Call a doctor!	¡Llame a un médico! *ya*·me a oon *me*·dee·ko

Fast Talk **Understanding Spanish**

Most sentences are composed of several words (or parts of words) serving various grammatical functions, as well as those that carry meaning (primarily nouns and verbs). If you're finding it hard to understand what someone is saying to you, listen out for the nouns and verbs to work out the context – this shouldn't be hard as they are usually more emphasised in speech. If you're still having trouble, a useful phrase to know is *¿Puede hablar más despacio, por favor?* pwe·de ab·*lar* mas des·*pa*·syo por fa·*vor* (Can you please speak more slowly?).

It's an emergency!	¡Es una emergencia!
	es *oo*·na e·mer·*khen*·sya
There's been an accident.	Ha habido un accidente.
	a·*bee*·do oon ak·see·*den*·te
Could you help me, please?	¿Me puede ayudar, por favor?
	me *pwe*·de a·yoo·*dar* por fa·*vor*
✂ **Please help!**	¡Ayuda por favor!
	a·*yoo*·da por fa·*vor*
I have to use the telephone.	Necesito usar el teléfono.
	ne·se·*see*·to oo·*sar* el te·*le*·fo·no
Where are the toilets?	¿Dónde están los baños?
	don·de es·*tan* los *ba*·nyos
I'm lost.	Estoy perdido/a. **m/f**
	es·toy per·*dee*·do/a

Police

Where's the police station?	¿Dónde está la comisaría?
	don·de es·*ta* la ko·mee·sa·*ree*·a
I've been raped.	He sido violado/a. **m/f**
	e *see*·do vyo·*la*·do/a
I've been robbed.	Me han robado.
	me an ro·*ba*·do
(My bag) was stolen.	(Mi bolso) fue robado.
	(mee *bol*·so) fwe ro·*ba*·do
(My money) was stolen.	(Mi dinero) fue robado.
	(mee dee·*ne*·ro) fwe ro·*ba*·do

I've lost (my passport).	He perdido (mi pasaporte). e per·*dee*·do (mee pa·sa·*por*·te)
I want to contact my embassy.	Quiero ponerme en contacto con mi embajada. *kye*·ro po·*ner*·me en kon·*tak*·to kon mee em·ba·*kha*·da
I want to contact my consulate.	Quiero ponerme en contacto con mi consulado. *kye*·ro po·*ner*·me en kon·*tak*·to kon mee kon·soo·*la*·do
I have insurance.	Tengo seguro. *ten*·go se·*goo*·ro

Health

Where's the nearest chemist?	¿Dónde está la farmacia más cercana? *don*·de es·*ta* la far·*ma*·sya mas ser·*ka*·na
Where's the nearest dentist?	¿Dónde está el dentista más cercano? *don*·de es·*ta* el den·*tees*·ta mas ser·*ka*·no
Where's the nearest hospital?	¿Dónde está el hospital más cercano? *don*·de es·*ta* el os·pee·*tal* mas ser·*ka*·no
I need a doctor (who speaks English).	Necesito un médico (que hable inglés). ne·se·*see*·to oon *me*·dee·ko (ke *a*·ble een·*gles*)
Can the doctor come here?	¿Puede visitarme el médico? *pwe*·de vee·see·*tar*·me el *me*·dee·ko

Negatives

To make a negative statement in Spanish, just add the word *no* no before the main verb of the sentence: *no hablo español* no ab·lo es·pa·nyol (lit: no I-speak Spanish). Contrary to English, Spanish uses double negatives: *no entiendo nada* no en·tyen·do na·da (lit: no I-understand nothing).

Could I see a female doctor?	¿Puede examinarme una médica?
	pwe·de ek·sa·mee·*nar*·me oo·na *me*·dee·ka
I'm sick.	Estoy enfermo/a. **m/f**
	es·*toy* en·*fer*·mo/a
It hurts here.	Me duele aquí.
	me *dwe*·le a·*kee*
I've been vomiting.	He estado vomitando.
	e es·*ta*·do vo·mee·*tan*·do
I feel nauseous.	Me siento con nauseas.
	me *syen*·to kon *now*·se·as
I feel breathless.	Tengo falta de aliento.
	ten·go *fal*·ta de a·*lyen*·to
I feel dizzy.	Me siento mareado/a. **m/f**
	me *syen*·to ma·re·a·do/a
I'm dehydrated.	Estoy deshidratado/a. **m/f**
	es·*toy* des·ee·dra·*ta*·do/a
I have a fever.	Tengo fiebre.
	ten·go *fye*·bre
I have a cold.	Estoy resfriado/a. **m/f**
	es·*toy* res·*frya*·do/a
	Tengo un resfrío. **(SAm)**
	ten·go oon res·*free*·o

Fast Talk

Body Language

You'll probably find that when you're talking with someone they stand closer to you than you're used to, and may touch you on the arm or shoulder. Acquaintances always greet with a *beso* be·so (kiss), and good friends often add an *abrazo* a·bra·so (hug). It's also fairly common to see people of the same sex walking down the street arm-in-arm.

I have a headache.	Me duele la cabeza. me dwe·le la ka·be·sa
I have a toothache.	Me duele una muela. me dwe·le oo·na mwe·la
I'm on medication for ...	Estoy bajo medicación para ... es·toy ba·kho me·dee·ka·syon pa·ra ...
I need something for (diarrhoea).	Necesito algo para (diarrea). ne·se·see·to al·go pa·ra (dee·a·re·a)
My prescription is ...	Mi receta es ... mee re·se·ta es ...
I'm allergic (to antibiotics).	Soy alérgico/a (a los antibióticos). **m/f** soy a·ler·khee·ko/a (a los an·tee·byo·tee·kos)
I have a skin allergy.	Tengo una alergia en la piel. ten·go oo·na a·ler·khya en la pyel

Dictionary

ENGLISH *to* SPANISH

inglés – español

Nouns in this dictionary have their gender indicated by Ⓜ or Ⓕ. If it's a plural noun, you'll also see pl. When a word that could be either a noun or a verb has no gender indicated, it's a verb.

- a -

accident accidente Ⓜ ak·see·*den*·te
accommodation alojamiento Ⓜ a·lo·kha·*myen*·to
air-conditioning aire acondicionado Ⓜ *ai*·re a·kon·dee·syo·*na*·do
airport aeropuerto Ⓜ a·e·ro·*pwer*·to
airport tax tasa Ⓕ del aeropuerto *ta*·sa del a·e·ro·*pwer*·to
alarm clock despertador Ⓜ des·per·ta·*dor*
antique antigüedad Ⓕ an·tee·gwe·*da*
appointment cita Ⓕ *see*·ta
arrivals llegadas Ⓕ pl ye·*ga*·das
art gallery museo Ⓜ de arte moo·*se*·o de *ar*·te
ashtray cenicero Ⓜ se·nee·*se*·ro
ATM cajero Ⓜ automático ka·*khe*·ro ow·to·ma·*tee*·ko

- b -

B&W (film) blanco y negro *blan*·ko ee *ne*·gro
baby bebé Ⓜ&Ⓕ be·*be*
back (body) espalda Ⓕ es·*pal*·da
backpack mochila Ⓕ mo·*chee*·la
bad malo/a Ⓜ/Ⓕ *ma*·lo/a
bag bolso Ⓜ *bol*·so
baggage equipaje Ⓜ e·kee·*pa*·khe
baggage allowance límite Ⓜ de equipaje *lee*·mee·te de e·kee·*pa*·khe
baggage claim recogida Ⓕ de equipajes re·ko·*khee*·da de e·kee·*pa*·khes
bakery panadería Ⓕ pa·na·de·*ree*·a
Band-Aids curitas Ⓕ pl koo·*ree*·tas

75

bank banco ⓜ *ban*·ko
bank account cuenta ⓕ bancaria *kwen*·ta ban·*ka*·rya
bath baño ⓜ *ba*·nyo
bathroom baño ⓜ *ba*·nyo
battery pila ⓕ *pee*·la
beach playa ⓕ *pla*·ya
beautiful bello/a ⓜ/ⓕ be·*yo*·a
beauty salon salón ⓜ de belleza sa·*lon* de be·*ye*·sa
bed cama ⓕ *ka*·ma
bedding ropa ⓕ de cama *ro*·pa de *ka*·ma
bedroom habitación ⓕ a·bee·ta·*syon*
beer cerveza ⓕ ser·*ve*·sa
bicycle bicicleta ⓕ bee·see·*kle*·ta
big grande *gran*·de
bill (account) cuenta ⓕ *kwen*·ta
birthday cumpleaños ⓜ koom·ple·*a*·nyos
black negro/a ⓜ/ⓕ *ne*·gro/a
blanket frazada ⓕ fra·*sa*·da
blood group grupo ⓜ sanguíneo *groo*·po san·*gee*·ne·o
blue azul a·*sool*
boarding house pensión ⓕ pen·*syon*
boarding pass tarjeta ⓕ de embarque tar·*khe*·ta de em·*bar*·ke
book libro ⓜ *lee*·bro
book (reserve) reservar re·ser·*var*
booked out lleno/a ⓜ/ⓕ *ye*·no/a
bookshop librería ⓕ lee·bre·*ree*·a
border frontera ⓕ fron·*te*·ra
bottle botella ⓕ bo·*te*·ya
box caja ⓕ *ka*·kha
boy chico ⓜ *chee*·ko
boyfriend novio ⓜ *no*·vyo
bra corpiño ⓜ kor·*pee*·nyo
brake freno ⓜ pl *fre*·no
bread pan ⓜ pan
briefcase maletín ⓜ ma·le·*teen*
broken roto/a ⓜ/ⓕ *ro*·to/a
brother hermano ⓜ er·*ma*·no
brown marrón ma·*ron*

building edificio ⓜ e·dee·*fee*·syo
bus (city) autobús ⓜ ow·to·*boos*
bus (intercity) ómnibus ⓜ *om*·nee·boos
bus station (city) estación ⓕ de autobuses es·ta·*syon* de ow·to·*boo*·ses
bus station (intercity) estación ⓕ de ómnibuses es·ta·*syon* de *om*·nee·boo·ses
bus stop parada ⓕ de autobús pa·*ra*·da de ow·to·*boos*
business negocio ⓜ ne·*go*·syo
business class clase ⓕ preferente *kla*·se pre·fe·*ren*·te
busy ocupado/a ⓜ/ⓕ o·koo·*pa*·do/a
butcher's shop carnicería ⓕ kar·nee·se·*ree*·a

- C -

cafe cafetería ⓕ ka·fe·te·*ree*·a
camera cámara ⓕ (fotográfica) *ka*·ma·ra (fo·to·*gra*·fee·ka)
can (tin) lata ⓕ *la*·ta
cancel cancelar kan·se·*lar*
car carro ⓜ *ka*·ro
car hire alquiler ⓜ de carro al·kee·*ler* de *ka*·ro
car owner's title papeles ⓜ pl del auto pa·*pe*·les del *ow*·to
car registration matrícula ⓕ ma·*tree*·koo·la
cash dinero ⓜ en efectivo dee·*ne*·ro en e·fek·*tee*·vo
cashier cajero/a ⓜ/ⓕ ka·*khe*·ro/a
change (money) cambio ⓜ *kam*·byo
change cambiar kam·*byar*
check (bill) cuenta ⓕ *kwen*·ta
check-in (baggage) facturación ⓕ de equipaje fak·too·ra·*syon* de e·kee·*pa*·khe
child niño/a ⓜ/ⓕ *nee*·nyo/a
church iglesia ⓕ ee·*gle*·sya
cigarette lighter mechero ⓜ

me·*che*·ro

city ciudad ⓕ syoo·*da*

city centre centro ⓜ de la ciudad
sen·tro de la syoo·*da*

clean limpio/a ⓜ/ⓕ *leem*·pyo/a

cleaning limpieza ⓕ leem·*pye*·sa

cloakroom guardarropa ⓜ
gwar·da·ro·pa

closed cerrado/a ⓜ/ⓕ se·*ra*·do/a

clothing ropa ⓕ *ro*·pa

coffee café ⓜ ka·*fe*

coins monedas ⓕ pl mo·*ne*·das

cold frío/a ⓜ/ⓕ *free*·o/a

comfortable cómodo/a ⓜ/ⓕ
ko·mo·do/a

company compañía ⓕ
kom·pa·*nyee*·a

computer computadora ⓕ
kom·poo·ta·*do*·ra

condom condón ⓜ kon·*don*

confirm confirmar kon·feer·*mar*

connection conexión ⓕ ko·nek·*syon*

convenience store tienda ⓕ de
artículos básicos *tyen*·da de
ar·*tee*·koo·los *ba*·see·kos

cook cocinar ko·see·*nar*

cough tos ⓕ tos

countryside campo ⓜ *kam*·po

cover charge precio ⓜ de entrada
pre·syo de en·*tra*·da

craft artesanía ⓕ ar·te·sa·*nee*·a

credit card tarjeta ⓕ de crédito
tar·*khe*·ta de *kre*·dee·to

currency exchange cambio ⓜ (de
dinero) *kam*·byo (de dee·*ne*·ro)

customs aduana ⓕ a·*dwa*·na

-*d*-

daily diariamente dya·rya·*men*·te

date (day) fecha ⓕ *fe*·cha

date of birth fecha ⓕ de nacimiento
fe·cha de na·see·*myen*·to

daughter hija ⓕ *ee*·kha

day día ⓜ *dee*·a

day after tomorrow pasado mañana
pa·*sa*·do ma·*nya*·na

day before yesterday anteayer
an·te·a·*yer*

delay demora ⓕ de·*mo*·ra

depart (plane etc) salir sa·*leer*

department store gran almacén ⓜ
gran al·ma·*sen*

departure (plane etc) salida ⓕ
sa·*lee*·da

deposit (bank) depósito ⓜ
de·*po*·see·to

diaper pañal ⓜ pa·*nyal*

dictionary diccionario ⓜ
deek·syo·*na*·ryo

dining car vagón ⓜ restaurante
va·*gon* res·tow·*ran*·te

dinner cena ⓕ *se*·na

direct directo/a ⓜ/ⓕ dee·*rek*·to/a

dirty sucio/a ⓜ/ⓕ *soo*·syo/a

discount descuento ⓜ des·*kwen*·to

doctor médico/a ⓜ/ⓕ *me*·dee·ko/a

dog perro/a ⓜ/ⓕ *pe*·ro/a

double bed cama ⓕ de matrimonio
ka·ma de ma·tree·*mo*·nyo

double room habitación ⓕ doble
a·bee·ta·*syon* *do*·ble

dress vestido ⓜ ves·*tee*·do

drink (beverage) copa ⓕ *ko*·pa

drink tomar to·*mar*

drivers licence carnet ⓜ kar·*net*

drunk borracho/a ⓜ/ⓕ bo·*ra*·cho/a

dry secar se·*kar*

-*e*-

each cada *ka*·da

early temprano tem·*pra*·no

east este ⓜ *es*·te

eat comer ko·*mer*

economy class clase ⓕ turística
kla·se too·*rees*·tee·ka

elevator ascensor ⓜ a·sen·*sor*

embassy embajada ⓕ em·ba·*kha*·da

English (language) inglés ⓜ

een·*gles*
enough suficiente soo·fee·*syen*·te
envelope sobre ⓜ so·*bre*
evening noche ⓕ *no*·che
everything todo *to*·do
exchange cambio ⓜ *kam*·byo
exhibition exposición ⓕ
ek·spo·see·*syon*
exit salida ⓕ sa·*lee*·da
expensive caro/a ⓜ/ⓕ *ka*·ro/a
express mail correo ⓜ urgente
ko·re·o oor·*khen*·te

-f-

fall caída ⓕ ka·*ee*·da
family familia ⓕ fa·*meel*·ya
fast rápido/a ⓜ/ⓕ *ra*·pee·do/a
father padre ⓜ *pa*·dre
fever fiebre ⓕ *fye*·bre
film película ⓕ pe·*lee*·koo·la
fine (penalty) multa ⓕ *mool*·ta
finger dedo ⓜ *de*·do
first class primera clase ⓕ
pree·*me*·ra *kla*·se
fish shop pescadería ⓕ
pes·ka·de·*ree*·a
floor (ground) suelo ⓜ *swe*·lo
footpath acera ⓕ a·*se*·ra
foreign extranjero/a ⓜ/ⓕ
ek·stran·*khe*·ro/a
forest bosque ⓜ *bos*·ke
free (gratis) gratis *gra*·tees
free (not bound) libre *lee*·bre
friend amigo/a ⓜ/ⓕ a·*mee*·go/a

-g-

gas (petrol) gasolina ⓕ ga·so·*lee*·na
gift regalo ⓜ re·*ga*·lo
girl chica ⓕ *chee*·ka
girlfriend novia ⓕ *no*·vya
glasses anteojos ⓜ pl an·te·o·*khos*
gloves guantes ⓜ pl *gwan*·tes

go ir eer
go out with salir con sa·*leer* kon
green verde *ver*·de
grey gris grees
grocer's almacén ⓜ al·ma·*sen*
guided tour recorrido ⓜ guiado
re·ko·*ree*·do gee·*a*·do

-h-

half medio/a ⓜ/ⓕ *me*·dyo/a
handsome buen mozo/a ⓜ/ⓕ bwen
mo·so/a
heater estufa ⓕ es·*too*·fa
help ayudar a·yoo·*dar*
here aquí a·*kee*
hire alquilar al·kee·*lar*
holidays vacaciones ⓕ pl
va·ka·*syo*·nes
honeymoon luna ⓕ de miel *loo*·na
de myel
hospital hospital ⓜ os·pee·*tal*
hot caliente kal·*yen*·te
hotel hotel ⓜ o·*tel*
husband esposo ⓜ es·*po*·so

-i-

identification identificación ⓕ
ee·den·tee·fee·ka·*syon*
identification card (ID) cédula ⓕ de
identidad se·doo·la de ee·den·tee·*da*
ill enfermo/a ⓜ/ⓕ en·*fer*·mo/a
included incluido/a ⓜ/ⓕ
een·kloo·*ee*·do/a
insurance seguro ⓜ se·*goo*·ro
intermission descanso ⓜ
des·*kan*·so
internet cafe cibercafé ⓜ
see·ber·ka·*fe*
interpreter intérprete ⓜ&ⓕ
een·*ter*·pre·te
itinerary itinerario ⓜ ee·tee·ne·*ra*·ryo

-j-

jacket chaqueta ① cha·ke·ta
jewellery joyería ① kho·ye·ree·a
jumper (sweater) chompa ⑩ chom·pa

-k-

key llave ① ya·ve
kind amable a·ma·ble
kitchen cocina ① ko·see·na

-l-

late tarde tar·de
laundrette lavandería ①
la·van·de·ree·a
laundry lavandería ① la·van·de·ree·a
leather cuero ⑩ kwe·ro
left luggage office consigna ①
kon·seekh·na
letter carta ① kar·ta
lift (elevator) ascensor ⑩ a·sen·sor
locked cerrado/a ⑩/① con llave
se·ra·do/a kon ya·ve
lost perdido/a ⑩/① per·dee·do/a
lost property office oficina ① de
objetos perdidos o·fee·see·na de
ob·khe·tos per·dee·dos
luggage equipaje ⑩ e·kee·pa·khe
lunch almuerzo ⑩ al·mwer·so

-m-

mail correo ⑩ ko·re·o
make-up maquillaje ⑩ ma·kee·ya·khe
man hombre ⑩ om·bre
manager director/directora ⑩/①
dee·rek·tor/dee·rek·to·ra
map mapa ⑩ ma·pa
market mercado ⑩ mer·ka·do
meat carne ① kar·ne
medicine medicina ① me·dee·see·na

metro station estación ① de subterráneo es·ta·syon de soob·te·ra·ne·o
midnight medianoche ①
me·dya·no·che
milk leche ① le·che
mineral water agua ⑩ mineral a·gwa
mee·ne·ral
mobile phone teléfono ⑩ móvil/
celular te·le·fo·no mo·veel/se·loo·lar
money dinero ⑩ dee·ne·ro
month mes ⑩ mes
morning mañana ① ma·nya·na
mother madre ① ma·dre
motorcycle motocicleta ①
mo·to·see·kle·ta
motorway autopista ① ow·to·pees·ta
mountain montaña ① mon·ta·nya
museum museo ⑩ moo·se·o
music música ① moo·see·ka

-n-

name nombre ⑩ nom·bre
napkin servilleta ① ser·vee·ye·ta
nappy (diaper) pañal ⑩ pa·nyal
newsagency quiosco ⑩ kee·os·ko
newspaper periódico ⑩
pe·ryo·dee·ko
next próximo/a ⑩/① prok·see·mo/a
night noche ① no·che
nonsmoking no fumadores no
foo·ma·do·res
north norte ⑩ nor·te
now ahora a·o·ra
number número ⑩ noo·me·ro

-o-

oil aceite ⑩ a·say·te
open abierto/a ⑩/① a·byer·to/a
opening hours horas ① pl de
apertura o·ras de a·per·too·ra
orange (colour) naranjo/a ⑩/①
na·ran·kho/a

-p-

painter pintor/pintora Ⓜ/Ⓕ peen·*tor*/ peen·*to*·ra

painting (art) pintura Ⓕ peen·*too*·ra

pants pantalones Ⓜ pl pan·ta·*lo*·nes

pantyhose medias Ⓕ pl *me*·dyas

paper papel Ⓜ pa·*pel*

party fiesta Ⓕ *fyes*·ta

passenger pasajero/a Ⓜ/Ⓕ pa·sa·*khe*·ro/a

passport pasaporte Ⓜ pa·sa·*por*·te

passport number número Ⓜ de pasaporte *noo*·me·ro de pa·sa·*por*·te

path sendero Ⓜ sen·*de*·ro

penknife navaja Ⓕ na·*va*·kha

pensioner pensionado/a Ⓜ/Ⓕ pen·syo·*na*·do/a

petrol gasolina Ⓕ ga·so·*lee*·na

phone book guía Ⓕ telefónica *gee*·a te·le·fo·*nee*·ka

phone box cabina Ⓕ telefónica ka·*bee*·na te·le·fo·*nee*·ka

phone card tarjeta Ⓕ de teléfono tar·*khe*·ta de te·*le*·fo·no

phrasebook libro Ⓜ de frases *lee*·bro de *fra*·ses

pillow almohada Ⓕ al·mo·a·da

pillowcase funda Ⓕ de almohada *foon*·da de al·mo·*a*·da

pink rosa *ro*·sa

platform plataforma Ⓕ pla·ta·*for*·ma

play obra Ⓕ *o*·bra

police policía Ⓕ po·lee·*see*·a

police station comisaría Ⓕ ko·mee·sa·*ree*·a

post code código Ⓜ postal *ko*·dee·go pos·*tal*

post office correos Ⓜ pl ko·*re*·os

postcard postal Ⓕ pos·*tal*

pound (money/weight) libra Ⓕ *lee*·bra

price precio Ⓜ *pre*·syo

-q-

quiet tranquilo/a Ⓜ/Ⓕ tran·*kee*·lo/a

-r-

receipt recibo Ⓜ re·*see*·bo

red rojo/a Ⓜ/Ⓕ *ro*·kho/a

refund reembolso Ⓜ re·em·*bol*·so

rent alquilar al·kee·*lar*

repair reparar re·pa·*rar*

return volver vol·*ver*

return ticket boleto Ⓜ de ida y vuelta (bo·*le*·to) de *ee*·da ee *vwel*·ta

road calle Ⓕ *ka*·ye

room habitación Ⓕ a·bee·ta·*syon*

room number numero Ⓜ de habitación *noo*·me·ro de a·bee·ta·*syon*

-s-

safe caja Ⓕ fuerte *ka*·kha *fwer*·te

sea mar Ⓜ mar

season estación Ⓕ es·ta·*syon*

seat asiento Ⓜ a·*syen*·to

seatbelt cinturón Ⓜ de seguridad seen·too·*ron* de se·goo·ree·*da*

service charge servicio Ⓜ ser·*vee*·syo

share (with) compartir kom·par·*teer*

shirt camisa Ⓕ ka·*mee*·sa

shoes zapatos Ⓜ pl sa·*pa*·tos

shop tienda Ⓕ *tyen*·da

shopping centre centro Ⓜ comercial *sen*·tro ko·mer·*syal*

short (height) bajo/a Ⓜ/Ⓕ *ba*·kho/a

show mostrar mos·*trar*

shower ducha Ⓕ *doo*·cha

sick enfermo/a Ⓜ/Ⓕ en·*fer*·mo/a

silk seda Ⓕ *se*·da

silver plata Ⓕ *pla*·ta

single (person) soltero/a Ⓜ/Ⓕ sol·*te*·ro/a

single room habitación Ⓕ individual a·bee·ta·*syon* een·dee·vee·*dwal*

sister hermana ① er·*ma*·na

size (clothes) talla ① *ta*·ya

skirt falda ① *fal*·da

sleeping bag saco ⓜ de dormir *sa*·ko de dor·*meer*

sleeping car coche ⓜ cama *ko*·che *ka*·ma

slide (film) diapositiva ① dya·po·see·*tee*·va

smoke fumar foo·*mar*

snack tentempié ⓜ ten·tem·*pye*

snow nieve ① *nye*·ve

socks calcetines ⓜ pl kal·se·*tee*·nes

son hijo ⓜ *ee*·kho

south sur ⓜ soor

spring (season) primavera ① pree·ma·*ve*·ra

stairway escalera ① es·ka·*le*·ra

stamp sello ⓜ *se*·yo

street calle ① *ka*·ye

student estudiante ⓜ&① es·too·*dyan*·te

subtitles subtítulos ⓜ pl soob·*tee*·too·los

suitcase maleta ① ma·*le*·ta

summer verano ⓜ ve·*ra*·no

supermarket supermercado ⓜ soo·per·mer·*ka*·do

surface mail por vía terrestre por *vee*·a te·*res*·tre

surname apellido ⓜ a·pe·*yee*·do

sweater (jumper) jersey ⓜ kher·*say*

swim nadar na·*dar*

swimming pool piscina ① pee·*see*·na

- t -

tailor sastre ⓜ *sas*·tre

taxi stand parada ① de taxis pa·*ra*·da de *tak*·sees

ticket boleto ⓜ bo·*le*·to

ticket machine máquina ① de boletos *ma*·kee·na de bo·*le*·tos

ticket office boletería ① bo·le·te·*ree*·a

time (hour) hora ① *o*·ra

time (period) tiempo ⓜ *tyem*·po

timetable horario ⓜ o·*ra*·ryo

tip (gratuity) propina ① pro·*pee*·na

today hoy oy

together juntos/as ⓜ/① pl *khoon*·tos/as

tomorrow mañana ① ma·*nya*·na

tour excursión ① ek·skoor·*syon*

tourist office oficina ① de turismo o·fee·*see*·na de too·*rees*·mo

towel toalla ① to·*a*·ya

train station estación ① de tren es·ta·*syon* de tren

transit lounge sala ① de tránsito *sa*·la de *tran*·see·to

travel agency agencia ① de viajes a·*khen*·sya de *vya*·khes

travellers cheque cheque ⓜ de viajero *che*·ke de vya·*khe*·ro

trousers pantalones ⓜ pl pan·ta·*lo*·nes

twin beds dos camas ① pl dos *ka*·mas

- u -

underwear ropa ① interior *ro*·pa een·te·*ryor*

urgent urgente oor·*khen*·te

- v -

vacant vacante va·*kan*·te

vacation vacaciones ① pl va·ka·*syo*·nes

validate validar va·lee·*dar*

vegetable verdura ① ver·*doo*·ra

view vista ① *vees*·ta

- w -

waiting room sala ① de espera *sa*·la de es·*pe*·ra

walk caminar ka·mee·*nar*
warm templado/a ⓜ/ⓕ tem·*pla*·do/a
wash (something) lavar la·*var*
washing machine lavadora ⓕ
la·va·*do*·ra
watch reloj ⓜ de pulsera re·*lokh* de
pool·*se*·ra
water agua ⓕ *a*·gwa
west oeste ⓜ o·*es*·te
when cuando *kwan*·do
where donde *don*·de
white blanco/a ⓜ/ⓕ *blan*·ko/a
who quien kyen
why por qué por ke

wife esposa ⓕ es·*po*·sa
window ventana ⓕ ven·*ta*·na
wine vino ⓜ *vee*·no
without sin seen
woman mujer ⓕ moo·*kher*
wool lana ⓕ *la*·na

~ *y* ~

yellow amarillo/a ⓜ/ⓕ a·ma·*ree*·yo/a
yesterday ayer a·*yer*
youth hostel albergue ⓜ juvenil
al·*ber*·ge khoo·ve·*neel*

Dictionary

SPANISH *to* ENGLISH

español – inglés

Nouns in this dictionary have their gender indicated by ⓜ or ⓕ. If it's a plural noun, you'll also see pl. When a word that could be either a noun or a verb has no gender indicated, it's a verb.

~ a ~

a bordo *a bor*·do aboard
abajo *a·ba*·kho below
abierto/a ⓜ/ⓕ *a·byer*·to/a open
abogado/a ⓜ/ⓕ *a·bo·ga*·do/a lawyer
abrebotellas ⓜ *a·bre·bo·te*·yas bottle opener
abrelatas ⓜ *a·bre·la*·tas can opener • tin opener
abuela ⓕ *a·bwe*·la grandmother
abuelo ⓜ *a·bwe*·lo grandfather
aburrido/a ⓜ/ⓕ *a·boo·ree*·do/a bored • boring
accidente ⓜ *ak·see·den*·te accident
acondicionador ⓜ *a·kon·dee·syo·na·dor* conditioner
adaptador ⓜ *a·dap·ta·dor* adaptor
aduana ⓕ *a·dwa*·na customs

aerolínea ⓕ *a·e·ro·lee·ne*·a airline
aeropuerto ⓜ *a·e·ro·pwer*·to airport
afeitadora ⓕ *a·fay·ta·do*·ra razor
agencia ⓕ **de viajes** *a·khen·sya de vya*·khes travel agency
ahora *a·o*·ra now
albergue ⓜ **juvenil** al·ber·ge khoo·ve·neel youth hostel
Alemania a·le·ma·nya Germany
alergia ⓕ *a·ler·khya* allergy
algodón ⓜ al·go·don cotton
alguno/a ⓜ/ⓕ sg al·goo·no/a any
almuerzo ⓜ al·mwer·so lunch
alojamiento ⓜ *a·lo·kha·myen*·to accommodation
alquilar al·kee·lar hire • rent
alto/a ⓜ/ⓕ al·to/a high • tall
amable a·ma·ble kind
amanecer ⓜ *a·ma·ne·ser* sunrise

83

ampolla ① am·po·ya blister
analgésicos ⓜ pl a·nal·khe·see·kos painkillers
Año Nuevo ⓜ a·nyo nwe·vo New Year
anteayer an·te·a·yer day before yesterday
antibióticos ⓜ pl an·tee·byo·tee·kos antibiotics
antigüedad ① an·tee·gwe·da antique
antiséptico ⓜ an·tee·sep·tee·ko antiseptic
apellido ⓜ a·pe·yee·do family name • surname
aquí a·kee here
arte ⓜ ar·te art
artesanía ① ar·te·sa·nee·a craft • handicraft
ascensor ⓜ a·sen·sor elevator • lift
asiento ⓜ a·syen·to seat
aspirina ① as·pee·ree·na aspirin
autobús ⓜ ow·to·boos bus (city)
avión ⓜ a·vyon plane
ayer a·yer yesterday

~ b ~

bailar bai·lar dance
bajo/a ⓜ/① ba·kho/a low • short (height)
baño ⓜ ba·nye·ra bath • bathroom • toilet
barato/a ⓜ/① ba·ra·to/a cheap
biblioteca ① bee·blee·o·te·ka library
blanco y negro blan·ko ee ne·gro B&W (film)
boca ① bo·ka mouth
boda ① bo·da wedding
bodega ① bo·de·ga liquor store • winery
boleto ⓜ bo·le·to ticket
— de ida y vuelta de ee·da ee vwel·ta return ticket
— sencillo sen·see·yo one-way ticket
bolígrafo ⓜ bo·lee·gra·fo pen (ballpoint)
bolso ⓜ bol·so bag • handbag

bosque ⓜ bos·ke forest
botella ① bo·te·ya bottle
brazo ⓜ bra·so arm
bueno/a ⓜ/① bwe·no/a good • nice

~ c ~

cabeza ① ka·be·sa head
cada ka·da each
cafetería ① ka·fe·te·ree·a cafe
caja ① ka·kha box
— fuerte fwer·te safe
— registradora re·khees·tra·do·ra cash register
cajero ⓜ **automático** ka·khe·ro ow·to·ma·tee·ko ATM
caliente kal·yen·te hot
calle ① ka·ye road
calor ⓜ ka·lor heat
cama ① ka·ma bed
— de matrimonio de ma·tree·mo·nyo double bed
cámara ① **(fotográfica)** ka·ma·ra (fo·to·gra·fee·ka) camera
cámara ① **de aire** ka·ma·ra de ai·re tube (tyre)
camarero/a ⓜ/① ka·ma·re·ro/a waiter
cambiar kam·byar change • exchange
cambio ⓜ kam·byo change (coins) • exchange
— de dinero de dee·ne·ro currency exchange
caminar ka·mee·nar walk
camisa ① ka·mee·sa shirt
camiseta ① ka·mee·se·ta singlet • T-shirt
cámping ⓜ kam·peen campsite
campo ⓜ kam·po countryside
cancelar kan·se·lar cancel
candado ⓜ kan·da·do padlock
cansado/a ⓜ/① kan·sa·do/a tired
cara ① ka·ra face
carnet ⓜ kar·net drivers licence
carnicería ① kar·nee·se·ree·a butcher's shop

caro/a ⓜ/ⓕ *ka·ro/a* expensive
carro ⓜ *ka·ro* car
carta ⓕ *kar·ta* letter
castillo ⓜ *kas·tee·yo* castle
catedral ⓕ *ka·te·dral* cathedral
cena ⓕ *se·na* dinner
centro ⓜ *sen·tro* centre
— comercial *ko·mer·syal* shopping centre
— de la ciudad *de la syoo·da* city centre
cerca *ser·ka* near • nearby
cerrado/a ⓜ/ⓕ *se·ra·do/a* closed • shut • locked
— con llave *kon ya·ve* locked
cerradura ⓕ *se·ra·doo·ra* lock (door)
cerrar *se·rar* close • lock • shut
chaqueta ⓕ *cha·ke·ta* jacket
cheque ⓜ *che·ke* cheque
— de viajero *de vya·khe·ro* travellers cheque
chica ⓕ *chee·ka* girl
chico ⓜ *chee·ko* boy
cibercafé ⓜ *see·ber·ka·fe* internet cafe
cigarrillo ⓜ *see·ga·ree·yo* cigarette
cigarro ⓜ *see·ga·ro* cigar
cine ⓜ *see·ne* cinema
circo ⓜ *seer·ko* circus
ciudad ⓕ *syoo·da* city
clase ⓕ *kla·se* class
— preferente *pre·fe·ren·te* business class
— turística *too·rees·tee·ka* economy class
coche ⓜ *cama ko·che ka·ma* sleeping car
cocina ⓕ *ko·see·na* kitchen • cuisine
cocinar *ko·see·nar* cook
cocinero/a ⓜ/ⓕ *ko·see·ne·ro/a* chef • cook
código ⓜ **postal** *ko·dee·go pos·tal* post code
comer *ko·mer* eat
comerciante ⓜ&ⓕ *ko·mer·syan·te* business person

comida ⓕ *ko·mee·da* food
comisaría ⓕ *ko·mee·sa·ree·a* police station
cómodo/a ⓜ/ⓕ *ko·mo·do/a* comfortable
cómpact ⓜ *kom·pakt* CD
compañero/a ⓜ/ⓕ *kom·pa·nye·ro/a* companion
compartir *kom·par·teer* share (with)
comprar *kom·prar* buy
con *kon* with
concierto ⓜ *kon·syer·to* concert
condición ⓕ **cardíaca** *kon·dee·syon kar·dee·a·ka* heart condition
conducir *kon·doo·seer* drive
consigna ⓕ *kon·see·nya* left luggage office
consulado ⓜ *kon·soo·la·do* consulate
corazón ⓜ *ko·ra·son* heart
correo ⓜ *ko·re·o* mail
— certificado *ser·tee·fee·ka·do* registered mail
— urgente *oor·khen·te* express mail
correos pl *ko·re·os* post office
corrida ⓕ *ko·ree·da* bullfight
cortar *kor·tar* cut
corto/a ⓜ/ⓕ *kor·to/a* short (length)
costar *kos·tar* cost
crema ⓕ *kre·ma* cream
— hidratante *ee·dra·tan·te* moisturiser
— solar *so·lar* sunblock
cuaderno ⓜ *kwa·der·no* notebook
cuando *kwan·do* when
cubiertos pl *koo·byer·tos* cutlery
cuchara ⓕ *koo·cha·ra* spoon
cucharita ⓕ *koo·cha·ree·ta* teaspoon
cuchillo ⓜ *koo·chee·yo* knife
cuenta ⓕ *kwen·ta* bill • check
— bancaria *ban·ka·rya* bank account
cuero ⓜ *kwe·ro* leather
cumpleaños ⓜ *koom·ple·a·nyos* birthday

-d-

dedo ⓜ *de*·do finger
defectuoso/a ⓜ/ⓕ de·fek·*two*·so/a faulty
demasiado (caro/a) ⓜ/ⓕ de·ma·*sya*·do (*ka*·ro/a) too (expensive)
derecha de·*re*·cha right (direction)
desayuno ⓜ de·sa·*yoo*·no breakfast
descanso ⓜ des·*kan*·so intermission
descuento ⓜ des·*kwen*·to discount
despacio des·*pa*·syo slowly
despertador ⓜ des·per·ta·*dor* alarm clock
después de des·*pwes* de after
detrás de de·*tras* de behind
día ⓜ *dee*·a day
diapositiva ⓕ dya·po·see·*tee*·va slide (film)
diariamente dya·rya·*men*·te daily
dinero ⓜ dee·*ne*·ro money
— en efectivo en e·fek·*tee*·vo cash
dirección ⓕ dee·rek·*syon* address
disco ⓜ *dees*·ko disk
dolor ⓜ do·*lor* pain
— de cabeza de ka·*be*·sa headache
— de estómago de es·*to*·ma·go stomachache
— de muelas de *mwe*·las toothache
donde *don*·de where
dormir dor·*meer* sleep
dos camas ⓕ pl dos *ka*·mas twin beds
ducha ⓕ *doo*·cha shower
dulce ⓜ *dool*·se sweet • candy
duro/a ⓜ/ⓕ *doo*·ro/a hard (not soft)

-e-

edificio ⓜ e·dee·*fee*·syo building
embajada ⓕ em·ba·*kha*·da embassy
embarazada em·ba·ra·*sa*·da pregnant
en en on • in
enfermero/a ⓜ/ⓕ en·fer·*me*·ro/a nurse

enfermo/a ⓜ/ⓕ en·*fer*·mo/a sick
entrar en·*trar* enter
enviar en·*vyar* send
equipaje ⓜ e·kee·*pa*·khe luggage
escalera ⓕ es·ka·*le*·ra stairway
escribir es·kree·*beer* write
escuchar es·koo·*char* listen
escuela ⓕ es·*kwe*·la school
espalda ⓕ es·*pal*·da back (body)
espectáculo ⓜ es·pek·*ta*·koo·lo show
esperar es·pe·*rar* wait
esposa ⓕ es·*po*·sa wife
esposo ⓜ es·*po*·so husband
espuma ⓕ **de afeitar** es·*poo*·ma de a·fay·*tar* shaving cream
esquí ⓜ es·*kee* skiing
esta noche *es*·ta *no*·che tonight
estación ⓕ es·ta·*syon* station • season
— de tren de tren railway station
— de autobuses de ow·to·*boo*·ses bus station (city)
— de ómnibuses de om·nee·*boo*·ses bus station (intercity)
— de subterráneo de soob·te·*ra*·ne·o metro station
estacionar es·ta·syo·*nar* park (car)
estómago ⓜ es·*to*·ma·go stomach
estudiante ⓜ&ⓕ es·too·*dyan*·te student
excursión ⓕ ek·skoor·*syon* tour
excursionismo ⓜ ek·skoor·syo·*nees*·mo hiking
explotación ⓕ ek·splo·ta·*syon* exploitation
extranjero/a ⓜ/ⓕ ek·stran·*khe*·ro/a foreign

-f-

facturación ⓕ **de equipaje** fak·too·ra·*syon* de e·kee·*pa*·khe check-in (luggage)
falda ⓕ *fal*·da skirt
farmacia ⓕ far·*ma*·sya chemist • pharmacy

fecha ① *fe*·cha date (day)
— de nacimiento de na·see·*myen*·to date of birth
fiebre ① *fye*·bre fever
fiesta ① *fyes*·ta party (celebration)
fotografía ① fo·to·gra·*fee*·a photo • photography
fotógrafo/a ⓜ/① fo·to·gra·fo/a photographer
frágil *fra*·kheel fragile
freno ⓜ pl *fre*·no brake
frío/a ⓜ/① *free*·o/a cold
frontera ① fron·*te*·ra border (frontier)
fumar foo·*mar* smoke

-g-

garganta ① gar·*gan*·ta throat
gasolina ① ga·so·*lee*·na gas • petrol
gasolinera ① ga·so·lee·*ne*·ra service station
gordo/a ⓜ/① *gor*·do/a fat
grande *gran*·de big
gran almacén ⓜ gran al·ma·*sen* department store
grifo ⓜ *gree*·fo tap • faucet
gripe ① *gree*·pe influenza
gris grees grey
guardarropa ⓜ gwar·da·*ro*·pa cloakroom
guardería ① gwar·de·*ree*·a child-minding service • creche
guía ① *gee*·a guidebook
guía ⓜ&① *gee*·a guide (person)

-h-

habitación a·bee·ta·*syon* room • bedroom
— doble *do*·ble double room
— individual een·dee·vee·*dwal* single room
hablar a·*blar* speak • talk
heladería ① e·la·de·*ree*·a ice-cream parlour

hermana ① er·*ma*·na sister
hermano ⓜ er·*ma*·no brother
hermoso/a ⓜ/① er·mo·*so*/a handsome
hielo ⓜ *ye*·lo ice
hija ① *ee*·kha daughter
hijo ⓜ *ee*·kho son
hombre ⓜ *om*·bre man
hombros ⓜ pl *om*·bros shoulders
hora ① *o*·ra time
horario ⓜ o·*ra*·ryo timetable
hoy oy today

-i-

idioma ⓜ ee·*dyo*·ma language
iglesia ① ee·*gle*·sya church
impermeable ⓜ eem·per·me·*a*·ble raincoat
incluido/a ⓜ/① een·kloo·*ee*·do/a included
informática ① een·for·*ma*·tee·ka IT
ingeniería ① een·khe·nye·*ree*·a engineering
Inglaterra een·gla·*te*·ra England
inglés een·*gles* English (language)
ir eer go
— de compras de *kom*·pras shop
— de excursión de ek·skoor·*syon* hike
isla ① *ees*·la island

-j-

jabón ⓜ kha·*bon* soap
joyería ① kho·ye·*ree*·a jewellery
juntos/as ⓜ/① pl *khoon*·tos/as together

-l-

lago ⓜ *la*·go lake
lana ① *la*·na wool
lápiz ⓜ *la*·pees pencil
largo/a ⓜ/① *lar*·go/a long

lavandería ① la·van·de·*ree*·a laundrette • laundry
lavar la·*var* wash (something)
lejos *le*·khos far
libra ① *lee*·bra pound (money/weight)
libre *lee*·bre free (not bound)
librería ① lee·bre·*ree*·a bookshop
libro ⑩ *lee*·bro book
limpio/a ⑩/① *leem*·pyo/a clean
llave ① *ya*·ve key
llegadas ① pl ye·*ga*·das arrivals
llegar ye·*gar* arrive
lleno/a ⑩/① ye·no/a full • booked out
Los Estados ⑩ pl **Unidos** los es·*ta*·dos oo·*nee*·dos USA
luz ① loos light

~ m ~

madre ① *ma*·dre mother
maleta ① ma·*le*·ta suitcase
malo/a ⑩/① *ma*·lo/a bad
mano ① *ma*·no hand
mapa ⑩ *ma*·pa map
maquillaje ⑩ ma·kee·*ya*·khe make-up
matrícula ① ma·*tree*·koo·la car registration • license plate number
medias ① pl *me*·dyas pantyhose • stockings
medio/a ⑩/① *me*·dyo/a half
mejor me·*khor* best • better
mercado ⑩ mer·*ka*·do market
minusválido/a ⑩/① mee·noos·*va*·lee·do/a disabled
mochila ① mo·*chee*·la backpack
monedas ① pl mo·*ne*·das coins
montaña ① mon·*ta*·nya mountain
motocicleta ① mo·to·see·*kle*·ta motorcycle
muebles ⑩ pl *mwe*·bles furniture
mujer ① moo·*kher* wife • woman
multa ① *mool*·ta fine (payment)
museo ⑩ moo·*se*·o museum
— de arte de *ar*·te art gallery

~ n ~

nada *na*·da none • nothing
nadar na·*dar* swim
nariz ① na·*rees* nose
navaja ① na·*va*·kha penknife
negocio ⑩ ne·*go*·syo business
— de artículos básicos de ar·*tee*·koo·los *ba*·see·kos convenience store
nieto/a ⑩/① *nye*·to/a grandchild
nieve ① *nye*·ve snow
niño/a ⑩/① *nee*·nyo/a child
no fumadores no foo·ma·*do*·res nonsmoking
noche ① *no*·che evening • night
nombre ⑩ *nom*·bre name
norte ⑩ *nor*·te north
noticias ① pl no·*tee*·syas news
novia ① *no*·vya girlfriend
novio ⑩ *no*·vyo boyfriend
nuestro/a ⑩/① *nwes*·tro/a our
Nueva Zelandia ① nwe·va se·*lan*·dya New Zealand
nuevo/a ⑩/① *nwe*·vo/a new
número ⑩ *noo*·me·ro number

~ o ~

objetivo ⑩ ob·khe·*tee*·vo lens
obra ① *o*·bra play (theatre) • work (of art)
ocupado/a ⑩/① o·koo·*pa*·do/a busy
oeste ⑩ o·*es*·te west
oficina ① o·fee·*see*·na office
— de objetos perdidos de ob·*khe*·tos per·*dee*·dos lost property office
— de turismo de too·*rees*·mo tourist office
ojo ⑩ *o*·kho eye
olor ⑩ o·*lor* smell
oreja ① o·*re*·kha ear
oscuro/a ⑩/① os·*koo*·ro/a dark
otra vez *o*·tra ves again
otro/a ⑩/① *o*·tro/a other

-p-

padre ⓜ *pa·dre* father

padres ⓜ pl *pa·dres* parents

pagar pa·*gar* pay

pago ⓜ *pa·go* payment

palacio ⓜ pa·*la·syo* palace

panadería ⓕ pa·na·de·*ree·a* bakery

pañal ⓜ pa·*nyal* nappy • diaper

pantalones ⓜ pl pan·ta·*lo·nes* pants • trousers

— cortos *kor·tos* shorts

pañuelo pa·*nywe·lo* handkerchief

— de papel de pa·*pel* tissue

papel ⓜ pa·*pel* paper

— higiénico ee·*khye·*nee·ko toilet paper

papeles ⓜ pl **del auto** pa·*pe·les del ow·to* car owner's title

paquete ⓜ pa·*ke·te* package • packet • parcel

parada ⓕ pa·*ra·da* stop

— de autobús de ow·to·*boos* bus stop (city)

— de taxis de *tak·sees* taxi stand

paraguas ⓜ pa·*ra·gwas* umbrella

parar pa·*rar* stop

parque ⓜ *par·ke* park

pasado ⓜ pa·*sa·do* past

pasajero/a ⓜ/ⓕ pa·sa·*khe·ro/a* passenger

pasaporte ⓜ pa·sa·*por·te* passport

pastelería ⓕ pas·te·le·*ree·a* cake shop

pastillas ⓕ pl pas·*tee·yas* pills

pecho ⓜ *pe·cho* chest

película ⓕ pe·*lee·*koo·la film (for camera) • movie

peligroso/a ⓜ/ⓕ pe·lee·*gro·so/a* dangerous

peluquero/a ⓜ/ⓕ pe·loo·*ke·ro/a* hairdresser

pensión ⓕ pen·*syon* boarding house

pensionado/a ⓜ/ⓕ pen·syo·*na·do/a* pensioner

pequeño/a ⓜ/ⓕ pe·*ke·*nyo/a small

perdido/a ⓜ/ⓕ per·*dee·*do/a lost

periódico ⓜ pe·*ryo·*dee·ko newspaper

periodista ⓜ&ⓕ pe·ryo·*dees·ta* journalist

pesca ⓕ *pes·ka* fishing

pescadería ⓕ pes·ka·de·*ree·a* fish shop

pez ⓜ pes fish

pie ⓜ pye foot

pierna ⓕ *pyer·na* leg (body)

pila ⓕ *pee·la* battery (small)

pintor(a) ⓜ/ⓕ peen·*tor*/peen·*to·ra* painter

pintura ⓕ peen·*too·ra* painting (art)

piscina ⓕ pee·*see·na* swimming pool

plancha ⓕ *plan·cha* iron (clothes)

plata ⓕ *pla·*ta silver

playa ⓕ *pla·ya* beach

plaza ⓕ *pla·sa* square

— de toros de *to·ros* bullring

policía ⓕ po·lee·*see·a* police

precio ⓜ *pre·syo* price

— de entrada de en·*tra·da* admission price

— del cubierto del koo·*byer·*to cover charge (restaurant)

primavera ⓕ pree·ma·*ve·ra* spring (season)

primero/a ⓜ/ⓕ pree·*me·ro/a* first

privado/a ⓜ/ⓕ pree·*va·do/a* private

probar pro·*bar* try (attempt)

productos ⓜ pl **congelados** pro·*dook·tos kon·khe·la·dos* frozen foods

profesor(a) pro·fe·*sor*/pro·fe·*so·ra* teacher • lecturer

prometida ⓕ pro·me·*tee·da* fiancee

prometido ⓜ pro·me·*tee·do* fiance

pronto *pron·*to soon

propina ⓕ pro·*pee·na* tip (gratuity)

pueblo ⓜ *pwe·*blo village

puente ⓜ *pwen·te* bridge

puesta ⓕ **del sol** *pwes·ta del sol* sunset

- q -

quemadura ① ke·ma·*doo*·ra burn
— de sol de sol sunburn
quien kyen who
quincena ① keen·*se*·na fortnight
quiosco kee·*os*·ko newsagency

- r -

rápido/a ⓜ/① *ra*·pee·do/a fast
raro/a ⓜ/① *ra*·ro/a rare
recibo ⓜ re·*see*·bo receipt
recorrido ⓜ **guiado** re·ko·*ree*·do gee·*a*·do guided tour
recuerdo ⓜ re·*kwer*·do souvenir
reembolso ⓜ re·em·*bol*·so refund
regalo ⓜ re·*ga*·lo gift
reloj ⓜ re·*lokh* clock
— de pulsera de pool·*se*·ra watch
reserva ① re·*ser*·va reservation
reservar re·ser·*var* book (reserve)
rodilla ① ro·*dee*·ya knee
ropa ① *ro*·pa clothing
— de cama de *ka*·ma bedding
— interior een·te·*ryor* underwear
roto/a ⓜ/① *ro*·to/a broken
ruidoso/a ⓜ/① rwee·*do*·so/a loud
ruinas ① pl *rwee*·nas ruins

- s -

sábana ① *sa*·ba·na sheet (bed)
sabroso/a ⓜ/① sa·*bro*·so/a tasty
saco ⓜ *sa*·ko coat
— de dormir de dor·*meer* sleeping bag
sala ① *sa*·la room
— de espera de es·*pe*·ra waiting room
— de tránsito de *tran*·see·to transit lounge
salida ① sa·*lee*·da departure • exit
salir con sa·*leer* kon date (a person)
salir de sa·*leer* de depart
salón ⓜ **de belleza** sa·*lon* de be·*ye*·sa beauty salon

sangre ① *san*·gre blood
sastre ⓜ *sas*·tre tailor
seda ① *se*·da silk
segundo ⓜ se·*goon*·do second (time)
segundo/a ⓜ/① se·*goon*·do/a second (place)
seguro ⓜ se·*goo*·ro insurance
sello ⓜ *se*·yo stamp
semáforos ⓜ pl se·*ma*·fo·ros traffic lights
sendero ⓜ sen·*de*·ro path
servicio ⓜ ser·*vee*·syo service • service charge
sexo ⓜ *sek*·so sex
— seguro se·*goo*·ro safe sex
silla ① *see*·ya chair
— de ruedas de *rwe*·das wheelchair
sin seen without
sobre ⓜ *so*·bre envelope
sol ⓜ sol sun
solo/a ⓜ/① *so*·lo/a alone
soltero/a ⓜ/① sol·*te*·ro/a single (unmarried)
sombrero ⓜ som·*bre*·ro hat
subtítulos ⓜ pl soob·*tee*·too·los subtitles
sucio/a ⓜ/① *soo*·syo/a dirty
suegra ① *swe*·gra mother-in-law
suegro ⓜ *swe*·gro father-in-law
supermercado ⓜ soo·per·mer·*ka*·do supermarket
sur ⓜ soor south

- t -

talla ① *ta*·ya size (clothes)
taquilla ① ta·*kee*·ya ticket office (cinema, theatre)
tarde *tar*·de late
tarjeta ① tar·*khe*·ta card
— de crédito de *kre*·dee·to credit card
— de embarque de em·*bar*·ke boarding pass
— de teléfono de te·*le*·fo·no phone card

tasa ① del aeropuerto *ta*·sa del a·e·ro·*pwer*·to airport tax

teatro ⓜ te·*a*·tro theatre

tele ① *te*·le TV

teléfono ⓜ te·*le*·fo·no telephone

— celular se·loo·*lar* cell phone

— público *poo*·blee·ko public telephone

templado/a ⓜ/① tem·*pla*·do/a warm

temprano tem·*pra*·no early

tenedor ⓜ te·ne·*dor* fork

tentempié ⓜ ten·tem·*pye* snack

tía ① *tee*·a aunt

tienda ① *tyen*·da shop

— de recuerdos de re·*kwer*·dos souvenir shop

— de ropa de *ro*·pa clothing store

— deportiva de·por·*tee*·va sports store

tijeras ① pl tee·*khe*·ras scissors

tipo ⓜ *tee*·po type

— de cambio de *kam*·byo exchange rate

toalla ① to·*a*·ya towel

tobillo ⓜ to·*bee*·yo ankle

todo *to*·do everything

torcedura ① tor·se·*doo*·ra sprain

toro ⓜ *to*·ro bull

torre ① *to*·re tower

tos ① tos cough

tostadora ① tos·ta·*do*·ra toaster

trabajo ⓜ tra·*ba*·kho work (occupation)

traducir tra·doo·*seer* translate

tranquilo/a ⓜ/① tran·*kee*·lo/a quiet

tranvía ① tran·*vee*·a tram

tren ⓜ tren train

turista ⓜ&① too·*rees*·ta tourist

- U -

universidad ① oo·nee·ver·see·*da* university

urgente oor·*khen*·te urgent

- V -

vacaciones ① pl va·ka·*syo*·nes holidays • vacation

vacío/a ⓜ/① va·*see*·o/a empty

vacuna ① va·*koo*·na vaccination

validar va·lee·*dar* validate

vaso ⓜ *va*·so glass (drinking)

venir ve·*neer* come

ventana ① ven·*ta*·na window

ventilador ⓜ ven·tee·la·*dor* fan (machine)

verano ⓜ ve·*ra*·no summer

verdulero/a ⓜ/① ver·doo·*le*·ro/a greengrocer

vestido ⓜ ves·*tee*·do dress

vestuario ⓜ ves·*twa*·ryo changing room • wardrobe

viejo/a ⓜ/① *vye*·kho/a old

volver vol·*ver* return

- Z -

zapatería ① sa·pa·te·*ree*·a shoe shop

zapatos ⓜ pl sa·*pa*·tos shoes

Acknowledgments
Associate Product Director Angela Tinson
Product Editor Kathryn Rowan
Language Writer Roberto Esposto
Cover Designer Campbell McKenzie

Thanks
Kate Chapman, Gwen Cotter, James Hardy, Indra Kilfoyle, Wibowo
Rusli, Juan Winata

Published by Lonely Planet Global Ltd
CRN 554153

2nd Edition – June 2018
Text © Lonely Planet 2018
Cover Image Havana, Cuba – Werner Bertsch/4Corners ©

Printed in China 10 9 8 7 6 5 4 3 2 1

Contact lonelyplanet.com/contact

Index

Q

R

T

U

V

S

W

INDEX

ABBREVIATIONS INDICATING COUNTRY-SPECIFIC TERMS USED IN THIS BOOK

Arg	Argentina	**Chi**	Chile	**Mex**	Mexico
Bol	Bolivia	**Col**	Colombia	**SAm**	South America
CAm	Central America	**Cub**	Cuba	**Ven**	Venezuela

10. Phrases to Get You Talking

Hello.	Hola. *o·la*
Goodbye.	Adiós. *a·dyos*
Please.	Por favor. *por fa·vor*
Thank you.	Gracias. *gra·syas*
Excuse me.	Disculpe. *dees·kool·pe*
Sorry.	Perdón. *per·don*
Yes.	Sí. *see*
No.	No. *no*
I don't understand.	No entiendo. *no en·tyen·do*
How much is it?	¿Cuánto cuesta esto? *kwan·to kwes·ta es·to*